The Malayan Emergency and Indonesian Confrontation

The Malayan Emergency and Indonesian Confrontation

The Commonwealth's Wars 1948–1966

Robert Jackson

Pen & Sword
AVIATION

First published in Great Britain in 1991 by Routledge
Printed in 2008
Reprinted in this format in 2011 by
PEN & SWORD MILITARY
an imprint of
Pen & Sword Books Ltd
47 Church Street
Barnsley
South Yorkshire
S70 2AS

ISBN 978 1 84884 555 8

A CIP catalogue record for this book is
available from the British Library

Printed and bound in Great Britain
By CPI UK

Pen & Sword Books Ltd incorporates the Imprints of Pen & Sword Aviation,
Pen & Sword Maritime, Pen & Sword Military, Wharncliffe Local History,
Pen & Sword Select, Pen & Sword Military Classics and Leo Cooper.

For a complete list of Pen & Sword titles please contact
PEN & SWORD BOOKS LIMITED
47 Church Street, Barnsley, South Yorkshire, S70 2AS, England
E-mail: enquiries@pen-and-sword.co.uk
Website: www.pen-and-sword.co.uk

CONTENTS

PREFACE

Between 1948 and 1966, British and Commonwealth forces fought two campaigns in South-East Asia, the first against Communist terrorists in Malaya, the second against Indonesian forces in Borneo. Both campaigns were concluded successfully, and had far-reaching consequences for the political stability of the Eastern Hemisphere.

The political background to both campaigns is complex and largely outside the scope of this work, which attempts to set out the military achievement in as concise a manner as possible, and to examine the lessons that were learned from it. A great many military units were involved in prosecuting both campaigns, and although some have been singled out for special mention it has been impossible to deal fairly with the achievements of them all, particularly in the context of the Malayan Emergency. A full list of military and air units involved will be found in the appendices to this book, together with a bibliography of recommended further reading.

RJ

Padang Besar
Kangar
THAILAND
Alor Star
KEDAH
Kota Bharu
PERHENTIAN
Betong
Yen
GREAT REDANG
PENANG
PROVINCE
Sungei
Patani
5035
Georgetown
Grik
6197
4982
Butterworth
Bayan
Lepas
PERAK
KELANTAN
Kuala
Trengganu
Taiping
7123
Port Weld
S. Siput
K. Marang
Matang
Ipoh
CAMERON
HIGHLANDS
TRENGGANU
Perak
DINDINGS
PAHANG
P. PANGKOR
Kuala Lipis
Telok
Anson
(Slim River)
6919
Jerantut
3462
Bagan Daton
Raub
Kuantan
Tranum
Mentakab
Tanjong Malim
Bentong
Temerloh
K. Kubu Bahru
SELANGOR
4799
Pekan
K. Selangor
Rawang
Kuala Lumpur
Pahang
NEGRI
TIOMAN
Klang
Bahau
Port Swettenham
Seremban
K. Langat
SEMBILAN
Rompiri
Telok Datok
Tampin
Gemas
Endau
Labis
Mersing
Port Dickson
MALACCA
Kluang
Yong Peng
JOHORE
Kota Tinggi
Kulai
Sembawang
SUMATRA
Bahru
Seletar
Changi
Tengah
SINGAPORE
© R.McN 90
MALAYAN EMERGENCY AREA OF OPERATIONS 1948-60
SCALE
0
20
40
60 MILES
Areas over 2,000 ft. in height
Railways

1

MALAYA: THE LAND AND THE PEOPLE

Malaya is one of the most beautiful, and at the same time one of the most primordial, countries on earth. In the north, the narrow Kra isthmus binds it to Thailand, its only land frontier; the peninsula itself is some 500 miles long, a little larger than England without Wales, ending at the Johore Strait which separates it from the island of Singapore. To the east, the South China Sea stretches away to the Philippines and the Pacific; to the west, beyond neighbouring Indonesia, lies the vast expanse of the Indian Ocean.

The hinterland of Malaya – more correctly known nowadays as Peninsular Malaysia – is largely inaccessible. The central mountain ranges, running like a spine along much of the country's length, rise to 7,000 feet at their maximum elevation. On their western, steepest side, rivers plunge down the mountain slopes in waterfalls and fast-flowing streams until they reach the 50-mile-wide coastal plain which faces Sumatra across the Malaccan Strait; on the eastern flank the slopes are gentler and the rivers longer and lazier, flowing into the South China Sea over palm-fringed beaches.

Carpeting the mountain ranges is the dense jungle, one of the oldest rain forests in the world. One hundred million years old, it covers four-fifths of the peninsula, together with its associated mangrove swamps:

> Harsh and elemental, implacable to all who dare to trifle with its suffocating heat or hissing rains, the jungle alone has remained untamed and unchanged . . . . Here the tall trees with their barks of a dozen hues, ranging from marble white to scaly greens and reds, thrust their way up to a hundred feet or even double that height, straight as symmetrical cathedral pillars, until they find the sun and burst into a green carpet far, far above; trees covered with tortuous vines and creepers, some hanging like the crazy rigging of a wrecked schooner, some born in the fork of a tree, branching out in great tufts of fat green leaves or flowers; others twisting and curling round the massive trunks, throwing out arms

like clothes-lines from tree to tree. In places the jungle stretches for miles at sea level – and then it often degenerates into marsh, into thick mangrove swamp that can suck a man out of sight in a matter of minutes . . . .

In an evergreen world of its own that will never know the stripped black branches of winter, elephants, tigers, bears and deer roam the thick undergrowth; flying foxes, monkeys and parrots chatter and screech in its high places; crocodiles lie motionless in the swamp; a hundred and thirty varieties of snake slither across the dead leaves on wet ground; the air is alive with the hum of mosquitoes ferocious enough to bite through most clothing; and on the saplings and ferns struggling to burst out of the undergrowth thousands of fat, black, bloodsucking leeches wait patiently for human beings to brush against them. Only on the jungle fringe is there colour and light and a beauty unmarred by fear. Here, when the sun comes out after a tropical shower, thousands of butterflies hang across the heat-hazed paths in iridescent curtains. Brightly coloured tropical birds dart like jewels between clumps of bamboo, giant ferns, ground orchids, flame of the forest trees, bougainvillaea, wild hibiscus, in a countryside heavy with the scent of waxen-like frangipani blossoms, where the occasional monkey watches suspiciously from the heights of a tulip tree with its clusters of poppy-red flowers.

(Noel Barber, *The War of the Running Dogs*)

This description of the Malayan jungle, by a man with first-hand experience of it over many years, is one of the best there is. It summarizes the contrasts of the wild, natural landscape that dominates every aspect of Malayan life. In its depths live the aboriginal tribespeople, shy folk who hunt small game with their blowpipes and who live in communal houses built on piles driven into the edge of a river near the plots of land where they cultivate their simple crops of rice, vegetables and sugar cane. Here, in their *kampongs* on the jungle fringes, close to the sea or the rivers, live the Mohammedan Malays, the indigenous people of the land, an attractive, courteous and endearing race who live their lives at a leisurely pace; they grow rice, breadfruit and papayas in and around their villages, harvest ginger, cinnamon and figs from the countryside's natural bounty, fish the abundant rivers and derive oil, roofing materials and coconuts from the palm groves.

The way of life of the Malays contrasts sharply with that of the Chinese. They are the town dwellers, and their lives revolve around commerce, although their influence has declined over the past forty years. In Singapore their influence is strong, but on the mainland, mainly because of the events described in this book, they have been ousted from posts of importance. Nevertheless, together with the Indian population of Malaysia, they continue to be a vibrant force in Malaysia's economic climate.

The Malays are an old race, probably the oldest in South-East Asia, at least in terms of civilization. Their origins are not clear, but they probably reached the peninsula from southern India by way of Sumatra. Long before the Christian era, they were carrying on a thriving trade in ivory, camphor, sandalwood and tin with merchants from the Coromandel coast of India and from China; by AD 160 they were known to the western world, and sixty years later, when gold was found in the peninsula, prospectors and adventurers arrived from many points of the compass, including the Roman Empire. The lure of gold attracted Indians in great numbers, bringing the Hindu religion with them and marrying into local families. In the fifteenth century Islam became the primary religion of Malaya, although the Hindu religion retained a strong following, particularly in the rich state of Kedah.

In the sixteenth century Kedah's main trade outlet was through the port of Malacca, which came under Dutch jurisdiction with the colonization of the East Indies a century later. The Dutch placed restrictions on all the ports within their sphere of influence, including Malacca, whereupon Kedah looked across the Bay of Bengal to Calcutta, where an English trading company had received its charter from Queen Elizabeth I on the last day of December 1599. Before long, the East India Company had set up a trading post at the mouth of the Kedah River, and England's long association with Malaya had begun.

Between 1765 and 1800, a series of treaties between the British and the Sultan of Kedah guaranteed the latter an annual income of several thousand Spanish dollars in exchange for British occupation of Penang Island and a strip of land on the coast opposite. One of the original conditions was that Britain would provide military aid for the Sultan if Kedah should be invaded by her powerful neighbour, Siam, but when the long-feared invasion came in 1821, resulting in Kedah being overrun and the population massacred, the British did nothing except provide sanctuary for the fleeing Sultan and his family. The failure to intervene seriously weakened British influence in Malaya for many years, even though an agreement engineered by the British led to a Siamese withdrawal from Kedah and parts of Perak, which had also been attacked, in 1826.

Siamese influence in Kedah remained powerful throughout the nineteenth century, and it was only with the approval of the Siamese Government that a British consul was appointed in the state in 1894 on the request of the Sultan. With the signing of the Anglo–Kedah Treaty of 1909, Kedah was brought directly into the British sphere of influence.

Meanwhile, the ports and settlements along the western coast of Malaya had been steadily prospering. Malacca had come under British influence in 1795, having been captured from the Dutch, and by 1825 the British foothold there was firmly consolidated. It was from Malacca, in 1811, that a British expeditionary force sailed for Batavia to take over the Dutch colonies in the East Indies; with it went a young man named Thomas Stamford Bingley Raffles, who was installed as Lieutenant-Governor of Java.

The fortunes of Malaya in the nineteenth century are indivisible from the name of Raffles. In 1818, he received a commission from the Governor-General of India to 'look for the establishment of a station beyond Malacca such as may command the Southern entrance of those Straits . . . and then . . . not the extension of any territorial influence, but strictly limited to the occupation of an advantageous position for the protection of our commerce'.

On 6 February 1819, a treaty was signed between Raffles and the ruler of Johore which granted the British the right to settle on Singapore Island. Raffles never lived to see the island and its port flourish under British rule, but by the middle of the nineteenth century it had achieved a high degree of prosperity, and in 1867 Singapore, together with the ports and settlements on the west coast of Malaya, became incorporated into the Crown Colony of the Straits Settlements. The British did not interfere in the affairs of the Malay States, but the strong British presence undoubtedly acted as a deterrent to potentially hostile external forces, so the states prospered in turn. Tin mines flourished in Perak, Selangor and Negri Sembilan, with a resulting influx of Chinese and Indian labourers in vast numbers, and new agricultural areas were established inland from the coastal communities.

Yet, as the century drew to a close, the whole economy of Malaya was threatened by inter-state division and rivalry among the Sultans. In some states, anarchy prevailed. The threat was recognized by the then Secretary of State for the Colonies, Lord Kimberley, who in September 1873 wrote to Sir Andrew Clarke, the new Governor of the Straits Settlements:

> Her Majesty's Government have, it need hardly be said, no desire to interfere in the internal affairs of the Malay States. But looking to the long and intimate connection between them and the British Government and to the well-being of the British Settlements themselves, Her Majesty's Government find it incumbent upon them to employ such influence as they possess with the Native Princes to rescue if possible, those fertile and productive countries from the ruin which must befall them if the present disorders continue unchecked . . . . I should wish you especially to

> consider whether it would be advisable to appoint a British Officer to reside in any of the States. Such an appointment could of course only be made with the full consent of the Native Government and the expenses connected with it would have to be defrayed by the Government of the Straits Settlements.

As a result of this initiative, the Treaty of Pangkor was signed on 20 January 1874 with Perak, Selangor and Sungei Ujong, followed in 1888 by Pahang. A British Resident was appointed to each state, and under his influence considerable progress was made in establishing law and order and introducing more modern ways to the states, which until then had been run on feudal lines. There were naturally mistakes and misunderstandings on both sides, and one British Resident was assassinated, but reason gradually prevailed and in 1895 the four states mentioned above were amalgamated under the First Federation, with central government in Kuala Lumpur. In 1910 Kedah, Kelantan, Trengganu and Perlis also signed treaties with Britain and accepted a Resident, followed by Johore – the most advanced state on the peninsula – in 1914. Tangible British assistance took the form of engineers, doctors and civil servants, and the state governments in Johore Bahru, Alor Star, Kota Bahru, Kuala Trengganu and Kangar dealt with the British High Commissioner through a Singapore Secretariat. At no time were the Malay States considered to be British territory, as were the Straits Settlements.

Under the advice of the British Residents and their staffs, the Malay States underwent a period of tremendous economic growth. Europe was now more readily accessible, following the opening of the Suez Canal in 1869, and a Malayan railway system began to be established in 1884. A British doctor, Malcolm Watson, campaigned vigorously for the clearance of swamps and streams in order to prevent the breeding of malarial mosquitoes; as a result of his efforts the disease was reduced to a fraction of its former level. Rubber replaced coffee as a major export at the end of the nineteenth century; before that the idea of growing trees to produce rubber had been greeted almost with scorn, but then the coffee crop was wiped out by blight, and the planters, faced with ruin, seized on rubber as their salvation. Most of the planters had come to Malaya from Ceylon and preferred to use Indian labour, so they imported Tamils and Sinhalese to tap the latex, using a method devised by Henry Nicholas Ridley, Director of the Straits Settlements Botanic Gardens. Before long, the great rubber estates were a leading feature of Malaya's ecology.

The years after the First World War saw more economic growth, with isolated communities linked by new roads, internal air routes established to link up with the magnificent Empire Airways routes that spanned half the world, and communications greatly improved through the establishment of radio stations.

By the late 1930s, Malaya was exporting annually a quarter of a million tons of rubber, two and a half million gallons of latex and eighty thousand tons of tin and tin ore, heading a long list of other products. Her economy was buoyant, and the happy relationship between the Federated Malay States and the British Empire seemed an enduring one. Apart from economic factors, the great base of Singapore was a cornerstone of British defence policy in the Far East.

The military planners of Imperial Japan recognized this fact too. And so did another enemy who, after the Japanese were driven from Malaya after three and a half terrible years of occupation, were to throw the land into bloody turmoil and draw the forces of the British Commonwealth into their most protracted war of the twentieth century.

2

THE COMMUNIST THREAT TO MALAYA

The Russian Civil War was barely over when, in the early 1920s, a Far Eastern Bureau of the Comintern – the Soviet organization for the dissemination of Communism outside Russia – was established at Shanghai. Chinese Communist agents quickly infiltrated Malaya and gained control of the emergent labour movement, and in 1929 the Malayan Communist Party (MCP) was formed with the intention of overthrowing the Malayan Administration and establishing a Communist-controlled democratic republic.

The MCP was highly subversive in its tactics and made powerful inroads into the schools and craft guilds of the Hainanese section of the Chinese community. However, it met with little response among the Malay population, which tended to be highly conservative. The MCP therefore concentrated in increasing its hold on the labour force, and in 1937 – by which time it had been made illegal – it was strong enough to foment a serious wave of strikes with the intention of crippling the economy of the country.

At the same time, events external to Malaya were beginning to have a significant effect on the outlook of the various elements of the Malayan Chinese community. In 1937, the Japanese renewed their attack on China, and this resulted in a truce being called between the Kuomintang and the Chinese Communist Party in order to present a united front against the invader. The Japanese aggression provoked strong patriotic feelings among the Chinese community in Malaya and the MCP was not slow to exploit these sentiments, forming anti-Japanese groups which attracted Chinese – and Malays – who were not interested in Communism but who might later be persuaded to join the cause.

When Great Britain became embroiled in war in Europe she received general support from the Malayan Chinese, with the exception of the Communist leaders. The latter continued to foment labour unrest, on the orders of Moscow, in order to embarrass the British war effort (so, as a matter of record, did members of the British Communist

Party, since Moscow and Berlin were then partners in the newly-signed non-aggression pact). This line later changed following the sweeping German victories in western Europe; fearful now of German aggression in the east, Moscow turned her attention more to potential new allies, and in 1940–1 the MCP swung round in support of the British. By this time the Kuomintang faction in Malaya, realizing that it was being engulfed by the MCP, had brought the uneasy alliance to an end and withdrawn its support.

The Communists now had an experienced underground organization in Malaya, with several thousand members. It was in an exceptionally good position to foment serious anti-British strikes and disturbances, and would undoubtedly have done so had it not been for Moscow's cautious tactics.

Early in December 1941, with a Japanese invasion of the Malay Peninsula seemingly imminent, steps were taken to establish a network of subversive agents who could operate against the Japanese from jungle bases if the country should be overrun. The only organization capable of undertaking this considerable task was the MCP, and, although the British Administration had misgivings about using it in this manner, there was no alternative. When Singapore fell at the close of a ten-week campaign, therefore, 165 key members of the MCP retired into the jungle to be trained in guerrilla tactics by a small number of British officers and NCOs.

It was this initial force that formed the nucleus of the Malayan Peoples' Anti-Japanese Army (MPAJA). As time went by its numbers were augmented by non-Communist Chinese who sought refuge in the jungle from Japanese persecution and who were soon indoctrinated. In the first year of the occupation the MPAJA enjoyed some initial success against the enemy, but by the beginning of 1943 it was critically short of arms, ammunition and other supplies and was in danger of being destroyed. In February 1943 British officers of Force 136, a Special Operations Executive (SOE) task force raised from former residents of Malaya and trained in Ceylon, were infiltrated into the peninsula to make contact with the MPAJA, to set up the necessary machinery for further deliveries of arms and ammunition by air and sea, and to direct the operations of the MPAJA when the time came for Allied forces to liberate the country.

During the last two years of the war, however, anti-Japanese guerrilla operations in Malaya were constantly hampered by a head-on conflict between the MPAJA and a rival guerrilla force, the Overseas Chinese Anti-Japanese Army (OCAJA), which had been raised and trained by the Kuomintang under the auspices of the Chinese Nationalist Government. After a protracted struggle the MPAJA gained the upper hand and forced the OCAJA into a small area of northern Perak, on the border with Thailand, and in the spring of 1945 the MPAJA once again turned its attention to the guerrilla war against the Japanese.

In fact, the MPAJA's activities during the summer of 1945 failed to produce any worthwhile results, even though SOE delivered 3,500 small arms and 500 trained fighters to assist the guerrillas during this period. By this time the MPAJA was a highly organized and well-armed force of some 4,000 guerrillas and 6,000 supporting personnel, mostly native tribesmen, deployed in seven independent groups. The whole force was under the leadership of Lai Tek, the Secretary-General of the MCP; during the planning for the re-conquest of Malaya (Operation ZIPPER), while appearing to give his full co-operation to the Force 136 operatives, he consistently refused to commit his forces to action. Neither did he reveal his political aims in the context of post-war Malaya.

The abrupt Japanese surrender in August 1945 spared Malaya the carnage and devastation of a major campaign. It also took the Allied authorities in South-East Asia and the MPAJA completely by surprise, but the latter were quick to recover and their 10,000-strong army emerged from the jungle and set about taking control of the country, setting up People's Committees in towns and villages and exercising intimidation through the ruthless use of 'traitor killing squads'. It was a time when Lai Tek might have seized complete power through a *coup d'état*; that he failed to do so was due in the main to divisions among the members of the MCP's Central Executive and Military Committees.

Meanwhile, the movement of the Commonwealth invasion forces that had been assembled in Indian ports for Operation ZIPPER was getting under way, and by the end of August large numbers of British and Indian troops landed in Malaya. In September a British Military Administration was set up in Kuala Lumpur, and by the middle of the month the BMA had deployed troops throughout the country to restore order. Malaya at this point was very close to collapse; although it had escaped the devastation of total war, there were acute food shortages, the economy was at a standstill, unemployment was widespread and disease and malnutrition were rife among the population. A wave of crime and disorder swept the peninsula, especially in the countryside, where the predominantly Malay police force had been used by the Japanese to support their operations against the MPAJA.

With the Japanese surrender there came a general collapse in police morale, resulting in most of the police force in the rural areas being withdrawn for screening and re-training. As a consequence, many rural areas had to be policed as a temporary measure by Commonwealth troops who were severely handicapped by their lack of local knowledge. They were unable to prevent MPAJA squads assassinating people, mainly Malays, who were suspected of working with the Japanese during the war. These actions led to inevitable reprisals by the Malays; in West Johore a situation developed between Malays and Chinese that was dangerously close to civil war, while in Negri Sembilan a Malay attack on a Chinese village killed forty people, most of them women and children.

With the help of the reorganized police force the British Military Administration set about clamping down on the activities of the MPAJA and MCP. The BMA refused to recognize the People's Committees, imposed restrictions on left-wing propaganda, disregarded the MCP's demands for political concessions and began the progressive disbandment of the MPAJA. All members of the various resistance movements were required to come forward and surrender their arms in return for a gratuity and a promise of rehabilitation in civilian employment; 6,800 did so and were officially disbanded at a series of military ceremonies, the MPAJA members parading in their British-supplied 'jungle green' uniforms. The BMA kept its word; each demobilized man and woman received 350 dollars (£45), a sack of rice and a job. The MPAJA also surrendered 5,497 small arms to the authorities, but succeeded in concealing a large number of other weapons which, unknown to the British authorities, they had seized from the Japanese after the latter surrendered. In addition, a hard core of 4,000 MPAJA guerrillas remained in being and went underground, ready to re-emerge and provide a fighting force for the MCP should the need arise.

There was no doubt about one matter: as a result of its anti-Japanese activities during the war, ineffectual though they might have been, the MCP was now the undisputed leader of Chinese nationalism in Malaya. The KMT was no longer a significant force in Malayan politics. What the Communists lacked at the beginning of 1946 was a firm policy for exploiting their new-found strength, and there was much disagreement among the MCP leaders about the right course of action to take. A sizeable majority advocated confrontation with the authorities, and early in January 1946 it was this faction which prevailed.

Following the arrest of thirty former guerrillas on criminal charges, the MCP called for a general strike throughout Malaya on 29 January 1946. It was successful, and virtually the whole country came to a standstill. However, a second general strike called for 15 February was not a success, thanks in the main to timely measures taken by the authorities.

In its attempts to strengthen and consolidate its position early in 1946, the MCP was aided by two main factors. One was the disaffection of large sections of the working population with conditions in general and continual food shortages in particular; the other was the confused state of Malayan politics in the immediate post-war years, which helped to divert the attention of the authorities from the growing Communist threat.

In 1945 the British Colonial Office had renewed its initiative, begun in the 1930s and interrupted by the Second World War, to bring about the unification of the Malayan States as a first step towards the independence of the nation as a whole. The proposal that emerged, in October 1945, was that the nine Malay States and the two Settlements of Penang and Malacca were to be merged in a single Malayan Union, but that Singapore was to remain a separate colony with its own governor. This would preserve Singapore's independent status as a developing free port, allow Britain to keep its important air and naval bases there, and keep the electoral potential of Singapore's one million Chinese at arm's length from a future independent Malaya.

The government of the Malayan Union was to be undertaken in the name of the British Crown, to which the Malay rulers of the nine States were to cede their sovereignty. All ethnic groups – Malays, Chinese, Indians and others – were to be eligible for citizenship of the Malayan Union so long as they were linked with Malaya by birth, or had been resident there for a prescribed period of time. They could also, if desired, retain their status as British, Chinese or Indian nationals.

It was a creditable enough plan; what was discreditable was the speed with which the British Colonial Office sought to implement it. No time was allowed for consultation between the rulers of the various states, nor to reconstitute individual State Councils, which had been inactive during the Japanese occupation.

Hardly surprisingly, the Malays reacted against it. So, too, did a number of influential Britons who had held high office in Malaya before the war. The Malays quickly took action by forming a political body, the United Malay Nationalist Organisation (UMNO); they elected a president and made an unofficial but dramatic protest by refusing to attend the installation of the first Governor of the Malayan Union, Sir Edward Gent, who took office on 1 April 1946.

The Colonial Office, realizing the nature of the blunder, immediately invited the Malay rulers and the UMNO to join in discussions with a view to working out a more acceptable form of constitution. From these talks there emerged a blueprint for a new Federation of Malaya, which was to be headed by a British High Commissioner. Each of the states was to have a chief executive and a deputy, both Malays, and an attached British Adviser with no executive powers. The Federal Government was to be carried on by the High Commissioner in the names of the Malay rulers jointly with the British Crown.

At the end of 1946 the proposals for a Federation of Malaya were referred to the Chinese, Indian and other non-Malay sections of the community for their reaction and comment. The plan was not well received, as it was seen to have a definite bias in favour of the Malays, and hostility to it became a matter of common cause between the middle-class Chinese and Indian communities, the Malayan Communist Party and other extreme left-wing movements.

Predictably, the Malayan Communist Party set about seeking allies from the other movements who were opposed to the proposed Federation, or rather to exclusive Anglo-Malay control of it. There were two such movements, namely the left-wing Malay Nationalist Party (MNP), which had strong ties with Indonesia, and the Malayan Democratic Union (MDU) in Singapore. In late 1946 the MDU, which was led by Chinese, Indian and Eurasian intellectuals, became the focal point of a political alliance styling itself the Pan-Malayan Council of Joint Action (PMCJA), which brought together a number of middle-class Chinese organizations and several Communist groups led by the MCP. For the latter, it was a golden opportunity to spread Communist dogma and influence among the higher social strata; that they failed in this was largely due to their insistence on continuing attempts to spread chaos through the country's economy by mass intimidation. The members of the MDU, however, were not the sort to take to the streets in open confrontation, and when it became clear that the British Government and the Malay rulers intended to proceed with their plan for a Federation of Malaya, a mood of political apathy gripped the middle-class opponents of the scheme and the PMCJA ceased to be an effective force – if, indeed, it ever had been one – in Malayan politics.

The Malayan Federation came into being on 1 February 1948, replacing the Malayan Union. During the preceding year the Malayan Communist Party had pursued its strategy of infiltrating trade unions; 277 of these were registered, and by the end of 1947 the MCP had gained control of 200 of them. The resulting organized labour unrest seriously affected an economy which was hard put to climb out of the depression resulting from the years of Japanese occupation, and it placed the MCP in a position of considerable strength – although it suffered one severe setback when, in March 1947, Lai Tek absconded and took the Party funds with him.

In February 1948, members of the MCP attended a Communist Youth Conference which was held in Calcutta. There, through Russian delegates, they received fresh instructions from Moscow. The Russians were planning a major political offensive in Europe; one of its aims was to squeeze the Western Allies out of Berlin, and other planned areas of confrontation were the Balkans and Italy. Soviet global strategy now looked towards fomenting unrest in the Far Eastern colonies of Britain and other European powers in order to divert attention and military resources from the European theatre. The MCP, in common with other Communist factions in South-East Asia, was ordered to go on the offensive.

The new Secretary-General of the MCP, Chin Peng (who, ironically, had been awarded the Order of the British Empire in 1945 for his wartime anti-Japanese activities), and his military commander, Lau Yew, set about organizing a Malayan People's Anti-British Army with a view to establishing a Communist republic in Malaya. This was to be achieved in four stages. First, Europeans were to be expelled from lonely rubber plantations and tin mines, many of which bordered the jungle; these attacks would also seriously disrupt the country's economy. At the same time, police and officials would be driven out of isolated villages. Second, 'liberated areas' would be set up under Communist control. Third, the Communists would expand outwards to link up the 'liberated areas' and extend their control to the larger towns and villages; and fourth, they would launch a general offensive against the British forces which they assumed would then be concentrated in the major administrative centres.

The offensive began at the end of February 1948 with a carefully orchestrated wave of violence, strikes and intimidation directed at all sections of the community. When this programme was thwarted by rigorous Government prohibitions, the campaign took a more vicious turn with the outbreak of a planned series of murders – including the killing of three European managers of rubber plantations at Sungei Siput in Perak – in the first week of June 1948. These outrages, together with associated acts of sabotage, were acclaimed in the Communist press throughout the world as a spontaneous expression of the suppressed peoples of Malaya rising from the yoke of British Imperialism.

By mid-June 1948, the scale of the insurrection throughout the Federation of Malaya called for the most drastic action. On 16 June, Emergency Powers were invoked by the Federal Government and the military authorities were called in to assist the civil administration in restoring law and order.

THE COMMUNIST TERRORIST ORGANIZATION

The Communist Terrorist (CT) structure in Malaya was organized along well-established lines, consisting of two main branches, one military and the other civilian. Both were controlled by the MCP, through a chain of command beginning with the Central Executive Committee and descending through the State Committees and District Committees to Branch and Sub-branch Committees. Members of the latter exercised political control over all military units, while the District Committees were responsible for the selection and co-ordination of terrorist attacks within their respective areas.

The total strength of the MCP at the start of the Emergency was about 12,500, of which an estimated 2,300 were actively engaged in military operations. Active terrorist strength rose steadily over the next three years, reaching a peak of 7,292 in 1951 and then steadily declining to only 564 in July 1960. At its peak, the terrorist force – which was renamed the Malayan Races Liberation Army (MRLA) on 1 February 1949 in a bid to gain popular support – was organized into eleven regiments deployed roughly on a State basis. Each regiment contained between 200 and 500 terrorists, divided between 4 or 5 companies and 10 or 12 platoons. Each regiment also had an Independent Platoon of 60 to 70 terrorists; these platoons acted in the main as mobile 'killer' squads.

In 1951 the CT Order of Battle was as follows:

No 1 Regiment (strength 220) assigned to Selangor
No 2 Regiment (strength 250) assigned to Negri Sembilan
No 3 Regiment (strength 250) assigned to north Johore and Malacca
No 4 Regiment (strength 370) assigned to south Johore
No 5 Regiment (strength 550) assigned to Perak and west Kelantan
No 6 Regiment (strength 380) assigned to western Pahang
No 7 Regiment (strength 150) assigned to south Trengganu
No 8 Regiment (strength 270) assigned to Kedah and Perlis
No 9 Regiment (strength 250) assigned to central Johore
No 10 Regiment (strength 100) assigned to central Pahang
No 12 Regiment (strength 460) assigned to north Perak and north Kelantan

The main concentrations of CTs were in the western States of Malaya, where the main centres of population were located. In the beginning, before they were forced to move into the jungle, most CTs were recruited locally and continued to live in their homes, emerging to take part in terrorist operations and then returning to live an outwardly normal life. This made it extremely difficult for the Security Forces to distinguish between them and innocent citizens, and the fear of savage reprisals initially deterred potential informers. By 1951, however, most CTs were concentrated in jungle hideouts, and the Security Forces had broken the back of the intimidation threat.

The CTs had a powerful support force in the form of the civilian branch of the Communist Terrorist Organization, known as the 'People's Movement' or 'Min Yuen'. In the peak years of the campaign the Min Yuen maintained essential supply lines to the CTs as well as providing recruits and an intelligence service. The Min Yuen's principal weapons were terror and intimidation, with which they controlled the so-called 'Masses Organization' which kept them supplied with food, clothing, money and medical supplies. By 1952, however, the position of the Min

Yuen was becoming increasingly precarious as the Security Forces began to get the measure of them, and in the mid-1950s most of them had gone over to active terrorist operations.

One of the main problems that beset the CTs after the early stages of the campaign was a shortage of weapons. Once the initial stocks of Japanese arms and ammunition were worn out or expended, the CTs had to rely on munitions captured from the Security Forces or stolen from Security Forces' depots. Partly because of an effective Security Forces' blockade of the Thai border, together with naval and air patrols that sealed off possible seaward supply routes from Indonesia, and partly because Communist China was heavily involved in the Korean War when the Emergency was at its height, the CTs were never able to obtain arms from external sources.

3

THE SECURITY FORCES

At the beginning of the Emergency, the Security Forces available for anti-terrorist operations comprised 9,000 Malay Police and ten infantry battalions. The bulk of the British Army garrison in Malaya in June 1948 was provided by the Brigade of Gurkhas, who had six battalions stationed on the mainland and a seventh on Singapore Island. There were also three British infantry battalions, divided between Singapore and Penang; the two on the Malay Peninsula were the 1st Battalion The Seaforth Highlanders and the 1st Battalion The King's Own Yorkshire Light Infantry. All seven Gurkha battalions had been deployed in Malaya and Singapore by March 1948 and were rapidly brought up to strength by the reserves of manpower available in Nepal (the Gurkhas having gone through a somewhat traumatic period of change when their battalions were divided between the British and Indian Armies after India gained her independence), but for some time they suffered from a shortage of experienced officers and NCOs to train them. In view of the fact that in the early days many young Gurkhas entered the jungle war without full training, the excellent record that was subsequently achieved by the battalions of the 1st Gurkha Rifles during the campaign was a great credit to this splendid fighting force.

Although the main task of the military forces – the pursuit and destruction of the MRLA – was difficult and dangerous enough, the task of the Federal Police, which was to protect the population from intimidation, was in many ways much harder, and the recruitment of manpower became of paramount importance. By the beginning of 1949 the number of Regular Police had risen to 12,767; a year later it was 16,220; in 1951 it reached 16,814; in 1952 it rose to 22,187; and in the following year it reached a peak of 36,737. From 1950 onwards the total included a Special Field Force of up to 3,000 men, whose task it was to man the deep jungle forts and patrol across the Thai border.

As well as the Regular Police there was a predominantly Malay Special Constabulary, which was some 10,000 strong in August 1948 and which reached a peak strength of 44,878 in mid-1952. The main task of the

Special Constabulary was to guard plantations, mines and other vital installations and to enforce food-control regulations, but by 1955 their role was changed to active patrolling by up to 600 Area Security Units and 40 to 50 Special Squads which operated outside their local areas. All Police units were controlled from the Federal Police Headquarters at Kuala Lumpur through State, District and Circle Headquarters, each of which included operational, CID and Special Branch staffs.

In 1949 a strong force of Kampong Guards, armed with shotguns, was formed to protect Malay villages from terrorist attack. An Auxiliary Police Force was also formed for traffic control and other duties in towns. At the end of 1950 the combined total of these two forces was 47,000, and their services meant that considerable numbers of Federal Police could be released to undertake more active operations. A Chinese Home Guard was also formed in September 1950, and in the following year this was amalgamated with the Kampong Guards as part of a restructured civil defence organization, providing a very considerable force of 300,000. At first it was not a particularly successful venture, because many of the Home Guards were Communist sympathizers and a substantial quantity of shotguns and ammunition found its way into CT hands. In 1955, after a rigorous screening process had eliminated unreliable members of the Home Guard and more areas were cleared of the Communist threat, the manpower was reduced to 152,000 and its strength continued to decline thereafter. In 1956, 8,500 Home Guards were assigned to active patrolling operations.

Other units under police command and control during the campaign were the Civil Liaison Corps, composed of Europeans and Chinese with local knowledge, whose members were attached to the Army to liaise with the local population, and the Special Operations Volunteer Force, which comprised ten platoons of former CTs who operated under the command of the Police Special Branch.

On the military front, reinforcements soon arrived in the shape of the 2nd Guards Brigade, which was composed of the 3rd Grenadier Guards, the 2nd Coldstream Guards and the 2nd Scots Guards. Other Army formations which arrived for service in Malaya subsequently, during the initial stages of the campaign, were the 1st Battalion The Queen's Royal Regiment (West Surrey), the 1st Battalion The Royal Lincolnshire Regiment, the 1st Battalion The Devonshire Regiment, and the 1st Battalion The Suffolk Regiment.

The number of Regular infantry battalions engaged in the Malayan campaign rose to 15 in 1949, and continued to rise until a peak of 23 was reached in 1953. Thereafter, 22 to 23 infantry battalions were retained on active service in Malaya until 1957, when the number was steadily reduced. In terms of personnel, the numbers rose from 10,000 in June 1948 to a maximum of 30,000, of whom half were non-operational. It was very much a Commonwealth effort; among the units serving in Malaya at the end of 1955 were six British, six Gurkha, seven Malay, one Fijian, one African and one Australian battalion, as well as a New Zealand squadron of the Special Air Service Regiment. All British battalions contained five companies and approximately 1,000 men. Much of the burden at the height of the campaign was borne by the Royal Malay Regiment, which fielded seven battalions.

Supporting the infantry at various stages of the campaign were two armoured car regiments, each containing up to six squadrons, one or two field batteries and one field regiment of artillery, two field engineer regiments, one Commando brigade, three squadrons of the 22nd Special Air Service Regiment and an Independent Squadron of the Parachute Regiment. Also operating in the infantry role was the Royal Air Force Regiment (Malaya), a locally-recruited force which fielded five rifle squadrons at the beginning of 1949.

COMMAND AND CONTROL

Up to April 1950 the campaign against the Communist terrorists was controlled by the Commissioner of Police, acting on the advice of members of the three Armed Services, but he had insufficient powers to ensure its effective direction. Lieutenant-General Sir Harold Briggs was therefore appointed Director of Operations to co-ordinate the activities of all security forces on behalf of the High Commissioner. The appointment was a civilian one; Briggs had retired from the Army, having commanded the Fifth Indian Division in Burma, and was persuaded to take on the task in Malaya by his friend Field Marshal Sir William Slim, then Chief of the Imperial General Staff. The original appointment was for a year, but in the event Briggs was to remain in Malaya for eighteen months.

Lieutenant-General Briggs directed operations in Malaya through the Federal War Council, whose members included the Chief Secretary of the Federation, the General and Air Officers Commanding in Malaya, the Commissioner of Police and the Secretary for Defence. From November 1950 the High Commissioner presided over the War Council, which assumed overriding powers in all matters affecting the Emergency.

Briggs was quick to realize that what was lacking in Malaya was a co-ordinated civil and military plan to fight and defeat the Communist terrorists. Even by April 1950, the extent of the Communist threat to Malaya was not fully appreciated by the British Government, which was slow to provide financial and military support to the degree that was needed to counter it effectively.

The formula devised by Briggs soon after his appointment – the so-called Briggs Plan – was to remain the keystone of anti-terrorist operations until the end of the Emergency. One of the most pressing problems that had to be dealt with was to isolate the enemy from all sources of supply and intelligence outside the jungle. In an attempt to achieve this aim the Federal Government had passed an Emergency Regulations Bill on 5 July 1948, giving the authorities sweeping powers that included the right to issue detention orders, declare protected or prohibited areas, seize property, control movement on the roads, disperse assemblies, impose curfews, control food distribution and impose severe penalties on any persons giving assistance to the terrorists.

In 1949, further regulations were promulgated which enabled the authorities to resettle squatter communities in areas that could be properly administered and policed. The squatter problem had existed since the 1930s and had been greatly aggravated during the Japanese occupation, when large numbers of unemployed Chinese had taken up land for food cultivation in order to support themselves and their families. Because they had no title to the land, these squatters usually chose to settle in remote and inaccessible areas on the fringe of the jungle. By 1948 there were an estimated 300,000 of them, and in the post-war turmoil the authorities had been unable to establish any measure of control over them. There was, however, a tendency to tolerate them because they were an economic asset, being self-sufficient and producing a surplus for sale in the towns, as well as providing a reservoir of labour for estates, mines and urban industries.

They also rendered considerable assistance to the Communist cause, either willingly or under duress, and in the first nine months of 1949, 6,343 of them were detained under the new regulations, 1,226 later being released and resettled in areas where they would not be subjected to Communist influence. Sometimes, whole villages known to have been consorting with the terrorists were detained. In addition, 9,062 people were repatriated to China in 1949, and a further 460 to India.

Under the Briggs Plan, Chinese squatters and others exposed to the Communist threat were moved to new settlements or regrouped in the same locality, the old settlements being replaced by 'New Villages' protected by barbed wire and a police station. By the end of 1950 over 117,000 people had been resettled in 140 New Villages which were defended by the Malay Police and the Chinese Home Guard. A year later there were 429 New Villages containing 385,000 people, and at the end of 1952 there were 509 such settlements with a population of 461,822.

The cost of the two-year resettlement operation was high – around 41 million dollars – and because of the speed with which it was carried out there was understandably widespread discontent at first. The sites of the New Villages were sometimes chosen with more regard to their defensibility than to agricultural and economic considerations, but as time went by the mistakes were gradually rectified. The squatters were given leases of land, some of the villages were provided with a piped water supply, electric light, schools, community centres and so on; the inhabitants were allowed to manage their own affairs, and for the first time the Chinese squatter was integrated into the Malayan political and social system. In the early 1960s, after the Emergency was over, 400 New Villages with a population of 300,000 were still in being as permanent settlements.

Apart from the squatters, the 60,000 Sakai aborigines who inhabited remote jungle areas of the central mountain range in Perak, Pahang and Kelantan were also subject to Communist intimidation, especially after 1952, when the activities of the Security Forces compelled the enemy to withdraw into the deep jungle. The Sakai provided the terrorists with labour for cultivating their food plots and acted as guides, porters and couriers. Most important of all, they provided an intelligence screen to warn the terrorists of the approach of Security Forces' patrols. To attempt to resettle the Sakai was considered to be both impracticable and politically unacceptable, and so in 1953 eleven deep-jungle forts were established to bring the Sakai under Government protection. The forts served as administrative centres, providing medical and trading facilities for the tribesmen. The scheme was a success; by the end of 1956 it was estimated that fewer than 400 Sakai remained under terrorist domination.

One of the most important steps taken by Lieutenant-General Briggs, in May 1950, was to establish a Federal Joint Intelligence Advisory Committee. The function of this was to co-ordinate all intelligence activities of the Security Forces and Civil Departments, to supervise the collation, evaluation and dissemination of strategic and tactical information, and to advise the Director of Operations on Emergency intelligence matters. A Director of Intelligence Services was appointed in August 1950, and by 1953 he was co-ordinating the work of what was now the Federal Intelligence Committee and the Combined Intelligence Staff, which included representatives of all agencies engaged in intelligence work in Malaya.

From 1951, this intelligence organization played a considerable part in enabling the authorities to implement a vigorous food denial campaign, which combined the disruption of the terrorists' supply lines with a sustained military effort to seek out and destroy their jungle cultivation plots. These measures were generally successful, forcing the terrorists to split up into smaller groups and progressively weakening their morale as starvation set in. In 1956, an Emergency Food Denial Organization was formed to supervise this campaign throughout the Federation.

In the first two years of the Malayan campaign the initiative lay entirely with the terrorists. There was no co-ordinated military and police plan of action for conducting operations against them, and the activities of both Army and Police were directed solely towards dealing with outbreaks of insurrection as and when they occurred. Only two carefully planned military operations took place during this period, both in 1949, when the Security Forces restored order in parts of Johore, but this success proved to be only temporary as the civil administration necessary to follow it up and maintain order was inadequate.

The Briggs Plan of June 1950 completely altered this state of affairs. Under a revised scheme, relatively small numbers of troops, working in close collaboration with the police, were deployed throughout the Federation to guarantee the population security against terrorist attack. Larger military forces were sent into the jungle to interdict terrorist supply lines, forcing the terrorists to risk contact if they tried to get their supplies through, or alternatively to flee to other areas. The overall plan envisaged beginning these so-called 'area domination' operations in Johore and then working steadily northwards to clear the Communist threat from other areas, the target date for the completion of operations being the end of 1950, but in the event the terrorists' foothold in Johore was much firmer than had been anticipated and the plan had to be revised. In the end, Malaya was progressively cleared of the terrorist threat from the central States outwards, and it was not until the end of 1958 that Johore was cleared. Communist-dominated areas were termed 'Black', and cleared areas 'White'.

The usual technique for offensive anti-terrorist operations involved a pre-planned combined operation designed to keep the enemy on the move by means of constant patrolling, the Security Forces being mostly supplied by air. The idea was to force the terrorists to split up into small groups that were easier to ambush, while food denial measures forced them to make contact with the civilian population, increasing the Security Forces' chances of eliminating them. In 1951 and 1952 the average length of an anti-terrorist operation was two months, but this was increased to at least three months in 1953 and subsequent operations were often protracted affairs lasting from six months to a year. It was these lengthy operations, which kept the enemy constantly on the move and denied them the necessary means of survival, which contributed in the main to their defeat.

The command and control organization during the early period of the Malayan Emergency suffered a number of serious setbacks. The first occurred on 2 July 1948, when Sir Edward Gent, the High Commissioner of the Federation of Malaya, was killed in an air crash during a visit to the United Kingdom. His successor was Sir Henry Gurney, who assumed the post on 6 October 1948. Gurney had been Chief Secretary in the last two years of the British Mandate in Palestine, and was therefore familiar with the ways of the terrorist.

A far-sighted man, Gurney recognized that the Emergency was first and foremost a struggle between ideologies, and that the first priority was to win the people of Malaya over to the anti-Communist cause. He declared that Communism would be fought on two fronts: on the first with the weapons of social, economic and political progress, and on the second by the Security Forces. It was Gurney who introduced amendments to the Emergency Regulations Bill, including the compulsory national registration scheme that required every man, woman and child over the age of 12 to register and carry an identity card. The assumption was that when registration was completed anyone not carrying a card could be presumed to be a terrorist or a Min Yuen accomplice.

On 6 October 1951, exactly three years after his appointment to the post of High Commissioner, Sir Henry Gurney was ambushed and killed by an MRLA unit on a bend on the Fraser Hill Road, about 40 miles north of Kuala Lumpur. The act was carried out by a force of thirty-eight insurgents who were subsequently hunted by the Security Forces for about a month. Five were killed, but the rest escaped. They included the insurgent leader Siu Mah, who survived in the jungle until he was shot dead by Security Forces on 9 March 1959, having been betrayed by two of his men as he was hiding in a cave near Ipoh.

The death of Gurney was a tremendous setback at a critical stage of the campaign, and there came another in the following month when Lieutenant-General Briggs had to resign from the post of Director of Operations because of ill-health. (He died in October 1952.) In January 1952 another leading figure in Malaya, Colonel W. N. Gray, the Federation Police Commissioner, also resigned. A tough former Royal Marine commando who had won the DSO and Bar in the European war, Gray had later been Inspector-General of Police in Palestine, and the anti-terrorist tactics he brought to Malaya with him in 1948 (along with some 300 former members of the Palestine Police) were not of the gentle kind. He remained a controversial figure during his time in Malaya and was not popular, but he did much for the police in the way of recruiting, organizing and obtaining equipment, including the creation of a first-class radio communications system.

A few weeks before Gray resigned, the Malayan theatre had been visited by Oliver Lyttelton (later Lord Chandos). A Conservative government had been returned to power, and Lyttelton was the new Secretary of State for the Colonies. A shrewd and capable man, Lyttelton toured the country and was disturbed by what he found. Morale was exceptionally low after the killing of Sir Henry Gurney; the civil administration was not geared up to what was clearly a war situation; the police were divided by internal schisms; there was a serious shortage of armoured and armour-protected cars for police patrols (Gray, in fact, had insisted that the police were not to travel in armoured vehicles, even in ambush-prone country, which had attracted bitter criticism from his colleagues); and angry planters were demanding greater protection and the implementing of a ruthless offensive against the terrorists. (The planters had a strong point: nearly one hundred of them were to be murdered before the end of the Emergency.)

In mid-December, Lyttelton broadcast a six-point programme to fight terrorism in Malaya, which included the centralized control of all military and civil forces, the reorganization of the police and the integration of Chinese into Home Guard units. Before the next High Commissioner was appointed, there was another matter to be attended to. Lyttelton asked for, and got, the resignation of Colonel Gray.

At the time of Lyttelton's visit to Malaya, the post of Director of Operations was filled by General Sir Rob Lockhart, who had taken over from General Briggs. The British Government, however, had a new man in mind for the post of both High Commissioner and Director of Operations in Malaya, although General Lockhart would stay on as Deputy Director of Operations and shoulder much of the burden. The new supremo in Malaya was General Sir Gerald Templer, who took up his dual appointment on 5 February 1952. A leader of considerable talent, Templer had a distinguished war record as a divisional commander. After the defeat of Germany he had been appointed Director of Military Government in the Western Zone, and he later became Director of Military Intelligence in the War Office. Templer's Deputy High Commissioner in Malaya was Mr (later Sir) Donald MacGillivray, who had been Colonial Secretary in Jamaica.

The British Government had vested Templer with the most extensive powers ever bestowed on any chief executive and commander-in-chief of a British dependency or protected state. One of his first acts was to issue a statement setting forth clearly the intentions of the British Government, of which he was the instrument of power. It began with a firm avowal on the part of the British Government that Malaya would in due course become a fully self-governing nation, and ended with the promise that Britain would not lay aside her responsibilities in Malaya until the Government was satisfied that Communist terrorism had been defeated and that partnership of all communities had been firmly established. To the Malayan people, it was an unmistakable message that Britain would not be forced into a situation whereby she relinquished her responsibilities in Malaya, as she had done in Palestine four years earlier.

After assessing the situation in Malaya, Templer set himself three priority tasks. The first was to reorganize the police and change its role from that of a para-military force to a more protective organization modelled on the lines of the British Police. To this end, Colonel (later

Sir) Arthur Young, Commissioner of the City of London Police, came to Malaya on a year's secondment to undertake the reorganization programme. Young initiated what was called 'Operation Service', which was designed to instil into the Federation Police a sense of service and courtesy to the community as practised in Britain. The object was to get the Malayan policeman, of whatever race, accepted as a helper and friend of the people, rather than as an oppressor.

Young set up training establishments throughout the country and founded a Police College for the more senior regular police officers. All police personnel were required to undergo an intensive training programme. They were equipped, at last, with armoured cars, reducing their casualties and improving confidence and morale as a result. Liaison between the police and the armed forces improved greatly. Recruitment figures rose steadily. By the end of Young's year in Malaya, the results of his efforts could be seen in a noticeable improvement in relations between the police and the populace, especially in rural areas.

Templer's second task was to create an efficient and centralized intelligence system. Much of the groundwork in this aspect had already been laid by General Briggs, who had realized that intelligence in Malaya was the Security Forces' Achilles' heel and had taken steps to remedy the situation. From 1948, most of the intelligence work in Malaya was carried out by the Special Branch of the Federal Police, which replaced an earlier organization called the Malayan Security Service. During General Briggs's tour the Special Branch had been reorganized by the Director of Intelligence, Sir William Jenkins, but his intentions had been thwarted by constant disagreements with Colonel Gray, and Jenkins had resigned after a year in the post.

General Templer brought in Jack B. Morton, second in command of MI5, to carry on Jenkins's work of reorganization, and a Malayan Police officer, Guy Madoc, was appointed Director of Intelligence. The Special Branch was segregated from the CID, although officers from the latter continued to be seconded to the former. A training school was set up in great secrecy in Kuala Lumpur, where officers were briefed on the objectives, formations and tactics of the MCP and its supporting organizations and given instruction in practical methods of obtaining and exploiting intelligence. Firm links were established with intelligence services in Thailand and other countries under Communist threat. The initial objective was to draw up an Order of Battle of the MCP, the MRLA and the Min Yuen and to compile lists of suspected Communist helpers and sympathizers.

Templer's third priority task was to initiate a psychological warfare campaign, designed as much to win the hearts and minds of the Malayan people as to intimidate the Communist terrorists. Details of how this was achieved will be found later in this book.

Another immediate step taken by General Templer was to increase the rewards being offered for the capture of Communist terrorists, alive or dead, by substantial amounts. The size of the awards ranged from $250,000 (about £30,000) for the Secretary-General of the MCP down to $2,500 for a rank-and-file terrorist. Sometimes, more drastic steps were taken to secure information; the case of Tanjong Malim was a classic example.

Tanjong Malim, on the Selangor–Perak border, was at the centre of a huge rubber-producing district with a population of 5,000, mostly Chinese. Between the beginning of January and the end of March 1952, CTs in the area carried out five ambushes and ten attacks on Army and police patrols, burned five lorries, slashed 6,000 rubber trees, attacked a Malay village and killed eight policemen and seven civilians, yet only on three occasions had people come forward with information. Templer summoned 350 Chinese, Malay and Indian leaders to a meeting in the town and informed them that, under the Emergency Regulations, he intended to impose a collective punishment on the community. He ordered the whole population of Tanjong Malim to be confined to their homes for twenty-two hours a day, being allowed out for two hours to buy food. He halved their daily rice ration, which had already been reduced to prevent supplies reaching the CTs, and said firmly that the restrictions would continue until the people were prepared to co-operate in ridding their district of the Communists. He also ordained that the town would cease to be the district capital until it had learned a sense of responsibility; in many ways, this loss of face was more seriously regarded by the population than the confinement or the reduced rations.

Finally, Templer issued a questionnaire about the local CT organization, which every adult was required to fill in. Twenty-four hours later, soldiers and police visited each house and collected the unsigned forms in sealed boxes. By the time the restrictions on Tanjong Malim were lifted a fortnight later, forty Chinese in the area had been arrested for being Communist food suppliers and couriers. Templer's methods were certainly unorthodox, but there was no doubt that they produced results.

General Sir Gerald Templer remained in command in Malaya until 1 June 1954, when he returned to the United Kingdom. He was subsequently promoted to Field Marshal and became Chief of the Imperial General Staff. His place as High Commissioner was taken by his former deputy, Sir Donald MacGillivray, while the post of Director of Operations was assumed by Lieutenant-General Sir Geoffrey Bourne, who was then General Officer Commanding, Malaya.

4

GROUND OPERATIONS: APRIL 1948 TO APRIL 1950

Before the declaration of the Malayan Emergency, the Security Forces were able to gain some experience in jungle warfare through two operations, PEPPER and HAYSTACK, which were mounted in the north Perak valley in May and June 1948. The objective was to clear the area of remnants of an anti-Communist Kuomintang faction calling itself the Malayan Overseas Chinese Self-Protection Corps, which, having set out to fight the Communists, had since discovered that brigandry was a more profitable pastime in an area where there was no Government control. The operations mounted against the bandits were under police control, with the support of Gurkha and Malay Regiment companies, and were not particularly auspicious. The main value derived from them is that they gave the Royal Air Force experience, for the first time since the end of the Second World War, in dropping supplies to patrols operating in the jungle.

Initial military operations following the declaration of the Emergency were undertaken by the six Gurkha battalions, three battalions of the Malay Regiment, the 1st Battalion The Seaforth Highlanders and the 1st Battalion The King's Own Yorkshire Light Infantry, soon to be reinforced by the three battalions of the 2nd Guards Brigade. In addition, No 91 Squadron of the RAF Regiment (Malaya) was operational in the Segamat area of Johore, working in conjunction with two companies of the Seaforth Highlanders. This composite force had considerable success in July 1948, arresting ten terrorist suspects and seizing large quantities of subversive literature.

Soon after the beginning of the Emergency, two special forces known as Ferret Force and Shawforce were formed to seek out terrorist camps in the jungle. Composed of fighting patrols of British, Malay and Gurkha troops, as well as police, these special forces were led by former Force 136 and Chindit officers who were fully conversant with jungle warfare. The special units had a fairly short existence, but they registered some notable successes. The most important was on 16 July 1948, when a special patrol ambushed and killed Lau Yew, the Chairman of the MCP's Military Committee and Commander of the MRLA.

The Special Force patrol, comprising fourteen Chinese and Malay detectives and led by a British officer, W. F. Stafford, located a hut in the jungle at the foot of a hill a mile outside Kajang, south of Kuala Lumpur. As they were approaching the hut they were seen by some women, who raised the alarm. The front door of the hut opened and three men dashed out, firing with revolvers as they scattered in different directions. A detective shot one man and killed him; he turned out to be Lau Yew. A second man was killed and the third captured. The detectives surrounded the hut and closed in. Inside, they found six women, one of whom was Lau Yew's wife, and handcuffed them. They also found maps, four rifles, three shotguns, three pistols and a sack containing 2,000 rounds of ammunition.

The police removed the women, and six detectives were sent back to the road with the arms and ammunition in order to summon transport for the prisoners and the bodies. The hut was set on fire and the Ferret Force patrol prepared to move off. At that point the police came under heavy fire from an estimated forty CTs firing with Bren guns from only 50 yards away. The police abandoned their captives, sought cover and returned the fire. Suddenly, the enemy stopped shooting and were seen to be withdrawing. Stafford, deciding to exploit the situation, led his men in a charge towards the CT positions, firing with their Stens and shouting in Malay and Chinese, 'Here come the Gurkhas!'

Stafford found that five of the women captives and the male prisoner had been shot dead, probably by the CTs to prevent them giving away information. Lau Yew's wife was gone, and so was her husband's body. Searching the area, the police found that they had killed three terrorists.

A few days later, Stafford and his police, acting on intelligence supplied by an informer, unearthed a huge arms cache six miles from Kajang. The haul comprised several dozen machine-guns, numerous Stens, 237 rifles and 10,000 rounds of ammunition in circular metal drums, just as they had been parachuted to Force 136 during the war. They had been buried in a dozen pits and young trees planted over them. Since the weapons had been intended for use by the MPAJA the Communists obviously knew all about them. The guns were all well oiled and in good condition. It was the biggest single arms haul of the anti-terrorist campaign.

The loss of Lau Yew was a serious blow to the CTs, and threw their combat organization into serious disarray. He was never replaced – indeed, there was no-one competent enough to replace him – and the Military Committee of the MCP gradually lapsed into disuse after his death. It has been argued that if the Security Forces had pursued a more vigorous campaign against the CTs in the late summer of 1948 the

Communist structure might have collapsed there and then; in fact, it was not possible to mount such a campaign at this juncture. Trained jungle troops were not yet available in sufficient numbers, and the accidental death of the High Commissioner, Sir Edward Gent, in July left a serious leadership gap that was not filled until October by the appointment of Sir Henry Gurney.

The man responsible for the conduct of the campaign against the Communist terrorists at this critical period was Major-General C. H. Boucher (later Sir Charles H. Boucher), the General Officer Commanding, Malaya. Boucher was an able enough commander and was conversant with Communist tactics and principles, having seen action against Communist guerrillas in Greece at the end of the Second World War. If he had a major fault it was perhaps over-confidence; he did not appreciate the Communist threat in Malaya to its full extent, and voiced the opinion that it would not be difficult to tackle.

Boucher's strategy was to use small, mobile forces to seek and destroy the CTs. It was a policy that often worked during the early weeks of the Emergency, while the MRLA was endeavouring to organize itself. Boucher has sometimes been criticized for his failure to meet the growing demand to station permanent garrisons in threatened areas of Malaya, but he would have found it difficult to do this with the resources at his disposal. Besides, the fact that his seek-and-destroy policy appeared to be producing results was encouraging. In one anti-terrorist operation in October 1948, for example, twenty-seven terrorists were killed and many more captured. In addition, twelve of their camps were destroyed in Johore.

Typical of the Security Forces' achievements during the autumn of 1948 was that of No 91 Squadron of the RAF Regiment (Malaya). By 4 September the Squadron had captured a total of sixty terrorist suspects on the Telok Sengat estate, bordering the Johore River, and later in the month, during a five-day jungle patrol, its men encountered a force of thirty terrorists and killed three of them for no loss.

Despite the reverses they were suffering, the CTs succeeded in intensifying their campaign as 1948 drew to a close, mounting vicious attacks on plantations, raiding villages, ambushing buses and other civilian vehicles. Among their targets were British troops, many of them National Servicemen, newly arrived in Malaya from the United Kingdom. By the end of the year the number of CT incidents was averaging fifty a week. Since the start of the Emergency there had been 1,274 incidents in all, resulting in the deaths of 149 members of the Security Forces and the wounding of 211 more. Civilian casualties amounted to 315 killed and 90 missing, while the terrorists themselves had lost 374 killed and 263 captured. In addition, a further 56 had surrendered voluntarily.

With the Security Forces substantially reinforced, the early weeks of 1949 saw the mounting of a series of offensive operations against one of the most active MRLA formations, No 5 Regiment, which was operating in the Cameron Highlands area of north-west Pahang and adjacent parts of Perak and Selangor. The first of these offensive operations, GARGOYLE, was carried out in January by the 2nd Gurkha Rifles, supplied by air. The air drops were generally satisfactory, but on one occasion the Gurkhas were robbed of an opportunity to ambush an occupied CT camp when the sound of supply aircraft alerted the CTs to the presence of Security Forces in the area and enabled them to carry out a successful evacuation.

In February 1949, Operation HOLIDAY was mounted on the northern borders of Kedah and Perlis in conjunction with the Thai police, the intention being to create a 'sealed belt' along the frontier to prevent Communist infiltration. The plan was hardly a success, and added greatly to the demand for air supply. In March, Operation NAWAB was launched against CT locations in central Kedah, and from April to July 1949 Operations RAMILLIES, BLENHEIM, SPITFIRE and SARONG maintained pressure on the 300 terrorists of No 5 Regiment MRLA in north Pahang and Kelantan. This large-scale series of operations was successful in that it drove No 5 Regiment northwards, and between July and September 1949 Operations PINTAIL, WIDGEON, PATHFINDER and OVERALL were mounted in Perak and Kedah to block the terrorists' escape routes. Meanwhile, Operations TRIANGLE, SNOW WHITE, LEMON and PLUNDER were mounted further south in south-west Pahang, northern Negri Sembilan and Selangor between April and September 1949, mainly against No 1 Regiment MRLA. The most notable success in these operations was achieved in April 1949, when the Security Forces eliminated 37 out of 45 terrorists in the Kuala Langat Forest Reserve area of Selangor.

Further successes were registered during Operations CONSTELLATION and LEO, which were mounted against No 3 Regiment MRLA in north-west Johore and Malacca in September and October 1949. The Security Forces killed 32 terrorists and captured 23, while 28 others surrendered. While these operations were in progress in central and southern Malaya, another operation, PUSSYCAT, was mounted in conjunction with the Thai police on the borders of Kedah and Perlis in an attempt to stop further infiltration and also to flush terrorists from the area. One more operation in 1949, LONDON, was carried out in Selangor with the object of disrupting the CT support force, the Min Yuen.

Tactically, the success of the Security Forces' operations during 1949 was due in large measure to the fact that the CTs persisted in operating in large units of up to 400 terrorists, which were far too unwieldy for rapid dispersal. The smallest MRLA formation at this time was No 10

Regiment, with 300 men, and this suffered particularly severely. Formed in Pahang from left-wing Malays and a sprinkling of Indians, it had been decimated by September 1949 and was later reformed as a predominantly Chinese unit.

By 6 September 1949, it seemed to the authorities that the back of the Communist revolt had been broken, and the Government decided to announce surrender terms for members of the MRLA. During the last three months of the year 116 CTs did in fact surrender under these terms, but it soon became apparent that most of these were Chinese who had taken to the jungle under coercion and who had quickly become disillusioned with the rigours of terrorist life.

The illusion that the MRLA was in confusion and on the retreat was soon dispelled. On 11 September, only five days after the surrender terms had been issued, the Communists launched a renewed offensive with an attack by 300 CTs on the town of Kuala Krau, in Pahang. They burned down the railway station, the houses of the station master and an inspector, and killed two British railway engineers. Then they attacked the police station, killing four policemen and two women, and derailed an armoured train that was heading to the relief of the town. On 4 October, 200 CTs of the same force attacked an isolated rubber estate in Pahang, burning the British manager's bungalow, the homes of the labourers and other buildings. Troops of the 1st Battalion The Devonshire Regiment were quickly moved into the area to restore order, but the terrorists had melted away into the jungle once more.

Between January and December 1949, 619 terrorists were killed, 337 captured and a further 251 surrendered. At the same time, 229 members of the Security Forces were killed and 247 wounded, while 334 civilians were killed and 200 wounded, with 160 more missing. The margin between CT losses and Security Forces plus civilian casualties – 1,207 against 1,107 – was therefore very narrow indeed, and there was every sign that the Communists, encouraged by Communist successes elsewhere in Asia, were making great efforts to improve their tactics and strategy in order to sustain their offensive.

The MRLA regiments began to divide their forces into smaller groups and to refine their ambush techniques against jungle patrols. They would, for example, plant sharpened bamboo stakes in the undergrowth along one side of a road and then ambush Security Forces' vehicles from the other side, so that troops seeking cover away from the fire would impale themselves. They dug carefully camouflaged pits on jungle trails and embedded bamboo spikes in the sides, designed to close on the body of anyone luckless enough to fall in and trap him in excruciating agony. They booby-trapped the trails with sacks filled with fifty pounds of sand into which iron blades were embedded; the sacks were then suspended over tree branches with a rope, the other end of which was fixed to a trip wire. When the first man in a patrol tripped the wire the sack swung back into the patrol, decapitating the second man and probably seriously injuring several others. All these techniques, and many others, were used later in Vietnam.

In the early weeks of 1950, jungle patrols became increasingly fruitless as the MRLA became more elusive, and the bulk of the Security Forces was withdrawn to guard towns and villages and to secure the ground between them. Most patrolling was carried out along the jungle fringes, where the terrorists normally contacted their Min Yuen supporters to receive supplies.

Despite the growing difficulty in making contact with the terrorists, the Security Forces managed to register some successes early in 1950. In January, for example, 25 CTs were killed by a patrol of the 1st Battalion The 2nd Gurkha Rifles during Operation THOR, which was mounted in the Yong Peng area of Johore, and in April, during Operation JACKPOT on the borders of Negri Sembilan, Selangor and Pahang, 29 members of No 2 Regiment MRLA were killed, 10 were captured, 15 surrendered and 74 Min Yuen accomplices were arrested. A second operation, CARP, which was mounted at the same time against No 5 Regiment MRLA east of Ipoh in Perak, was much less successful.

Although it was suspected that terrorist groups had been compelled to change their location, no contact was made with them. However, three more operations, THANDIANI, BAXUAL and BUTLIN, which were mounted in the Jerantut and Sungei Sembing areas of Pahang in the first three months of 1950, resulted in the elimination of at least thirty terrorists.

One of the most successful operations, but also the most costly in terms of Security Forces' casualties, during this phase of the anti-terrorist campaign occurred late in March 1950. On 23 March, a scouting platoon from D Company, 3rd Battalion The Malay Regiment, set out from its base at Pulai for a routine three-day patrol in Kelantan. Accompanying the platoon were sixteen special constables who were escorting Chinese villagers to collect attap a few hours' march away.

The platoon completed the first day of its patrol, spent the night in the jungle and then returned to join the attap-gatherers, with whom the soldiers spent a second night. The next morning, the soldiers broke camp and set off to follow the Semur River back to Pulai, 8 miles distant over rugged terrain. The special constables were left with instructions to escort the Chinese back to Pulai independently when the villagers had finished their work.

An hour and a half later, the platoon, which was spread out over 150 yards and following a narrow, uneven track on the exposed south bank of the Semur, came under heavy fire from the opposite bank, where terrorists had been lying in wait in shallow, camouflaged foxholes along a 350-yard line. A crossing further down the river was covered by terrorist positions on two small hills, and there were more enemy positions on the wooded slopes above the south bank, so that the whole of the platoon's path was covered by fire from short range.

The first bursts of enemy fire killed several soldiers, including the platoon commander, 2nd Lieutenant Hassan bin Haji Yassin. Command was assumed by Corporal Jamaluddin bin Mohamed, who ordered the mortar section into action. It managed to get off two rounds before it was knocked out. Together with another soldier, Jamaluddin attempted to engage the CT positions on the southern slopes while the rest of the platoon engaged those across the river, which was about 30 yards wide at this point, but they were pinned down by enemy fire.

The corporal ordered his men to cease fire in order to conserve ammunition, and in the ensuing lull the Communists made shouted demands for the surviving soldiers to surrender. One of the enemy who was shouting the surrender demands showed himself briefly, and was at once shot dead. Three more rushed from their positions to retrieve him, and they too were shot down. Three others tried to rush Jamaluddin's position, and were killed at 15 yards range by the corporal and his companion.

The fighting went on sporadically, the CT demands for surrender alternating with more bursts of heavy fire. Meanwhile, the shooting had been heard by the NCO in charge of the Chinese villagers, Police Sergeant Wan Yaacob, who had told the Chinese to stay where they were and set out with his fifteen men to relieve the embattled platoon. On reaching the scene, Wan Yaacob despatched his Bren section of seven men to create a diversion at the river-crossing downstream; the section tried to get across but only three men succeeded.

Wan Yaacob and his remaining eight men then tried to outflank the CT positions, firing whenever a target showed itself. They killed at least one Communist who was carrying a Bren gun. Then, on the opposite bank, a group of CTs rushed Corporal Jamaluddin and the soldier who was with him and killed them.

It was effectively the end of the platoon's resistance. Fifteen soldiers were dead, and three others so badly wounded that they died later. Six more had also sustained wounds. Only three men had escaped unharmed.

Wan Yaacob and the eight men with him took cover in the jungle and got away under cover of darkness, reaching Pulai the following morning. Meanwhile, the CTs had rounded up the seven police who had tried to cross the river and assembled them on the north bank, together with the wounded. The Chinese villagers, who came along the river on rafts later, were also apprehended. All the prisoners were questioned, then lectured on their folly in fighting the MRLA. After that, to their astonishment, they were released and the CTs vanished into the jungle. The survivors boarded the rafts and floated downstream towards Pulai.

Two days later, Malay Regiment troops and police from Kota Bahru and Pulai visited the scene of the battle. They found that the CT foxholes had been turned into makeshift graves, each containing the bodies of one or more terrorists. Twenty-nine CTs had been killed; no-one ever found out how many more had been wounded, perhaps to die in the jungle. Never again, during all the long years of the Emergency, would so many terrorists be eliminated in a single engagement.

5

GROUND OPERATIONS PHASE TWO: APRIL 1950 TO DECEMBER 1951

In terms of actual contact with the terrorists, many of the Security Forces' operations mounted between May and December 1950 proved abortive. During Operations CARP, ALBEMARLE, RABBIT and CLEAVER II, mounted during this period against No 5 Regiment MRLA in Perak, troops and police spent months of fruitless patrolling without making contact with the enemy.

Operations in other areas, however, met with more success. In August, Operation MOCCASIN, which was mounted in Johore, resulted in thirty terrorist eliminations, while Operation ASBAB in the Yong Peng area brought about the arrest of sixty-two Min Yuen. Operations KOHAT, JACKAL and LETTER, mounted between October and December 1950, seriously disrupted the 6th Company of No 4 Regiment MRLA, while a second seek-and-destroy operation, AUTUMN DOUBLE, in the border area of Negri Sembilan, Selangor and Pahang during October caused further losses in the ranks of No 2 Regiment MRLA, eleven terrorists being killed and seventeen of their camps destroyed. Operation ROSE against elements of No 8 Regiment MRLA in the Kulim area of Kedah proved abortive in September, but three operations on the eastern side of the Federation, WALKOVER and TREK in Trengganu and KOTA in Kelantan led to the destruction of a number of terrorist cultivation plots. Following these operations, local Home Guard units were established in the operational areas.

By the end of 1950, sustained pressure by the Security Forces had compelled the MRLA to split into smaller groups. In terms of casualty statistics, however, the terrorists held the upper hand. During the year, the Security Forces had killed 648 terrorists and captured 147, with a further 147 surrendering, but on the debit side the Security Forces had lost 393 killed and 496 wounded, while civilian casualties amounted to 646 dead, 409 wounded and 106 missing.

The year 1951 was to prove crucial in the campaign against the terrorists, who now launched an all-out effort to disrupt the Briggs Plan. Two and a half years of anti-terrorist operations had greatly improved the Security Forces' tactics and their intelligence had also improved, increasing the chances of making contact with the enemy. The year got off to an inauspicious start when Operations KICK OFF, CATHEDRAL and HUSTLE in south-west Pahang, Selangor and Negri Sembilan in January failed to make contact with the CTs, but in February six terrorists of the 24th Company, No 6 Regiment MRLA were killed during Operation STYMIE, which was mounted in the Raub area of Pahang, and six more CTs of the 28th Company of the same regiment were killed near Temerloh during Operation SABAI in the following month, these eliminations being achieved by Gurkha patrols.

Also in February and March 1951, Operations VALETTA, MANTRAP and TANSING in the Rawang and Bentong areas of Selangor and Pahang resulted in the killing of six terrorists and the dispersal of a force exceeding 250 in strength.

From March 1951 onwards, the formation of Police Jungle Companies under the Briggs Plan enabled the Army to progressively hand over its commitment in the whole of Kelantan and the Kuantan area of east Pahang, releasing troops for operations in other areas. In March, strong pressure was put on the MRLA in the Labis area of Johore during Operations DAGGER and TARGET, and in the same month Operation PROSAIC was mounted in south-east Pahang.

The latter operation was notable in that it saw the use, for the first time in Malaya, of Special Air Service troops for deep-jungle penetrations. The history of the SAS involvement in Malaya dated from the previous year, when Brigadier J. M. Calvert, who had commanded the SAS Brigade during the closing stages of the Second World War and who was a staff officer in Hong Kong in 1950, was summoned to Malaya by General Sir John (later Field Marshal Lord) Harding, Commander-in-Chief of Far East Land Forces. Calvert (who since the war had reverted to his substantive rank of Major) was briefed to study the situation in Malaya and make recommendations on how to tackle the problem of eliminating the CTs in their deep-jungle hideouts.

Calvert spent six months on a fact-finding tour of Malaya, spending time with infantry patrols and making lengthy journeys through Communist-threatened areas. Apart from other recommendations – which included the removal of squatters from the jungle fringes and their enclosure in defended villages – he suggested the formation of a special force to harass the enemy in the deep jungle and also to cultivate the friendship of the Sakai tribesmen.

The outcome of Calvert's report was that he was authorized to form a special force known as the Malayan Scouts (SAS), which in 1952 was to form the nucleus of the 22nd Special Air Service Regiment. The A Squadron was composed of local volunteers, some of whom proved to be heavy drinkers and therefore unsatisfactory for the job in hand, but others were excellent material, having served in Force 136 and Ferret Force. B Squadron was made up of volunteers from 21 SAS (Artists) TA, a Territorial regiment formed in 1947 which took its title as the result of a merger with the Artists' Rifles. M Troop of 21 SAS (Artists) had been preparing for service in Korea when it was diverted to Malaya, where it became B Squadron of the Malayan Scouts.

Calvert also visited Rhodesia to recruit volunteers. Out of 1,000 men who came forward, he and his staff were able to select 120 suitable candidates to form C Squadron. A fourth squadron, D, was also formed before Calvert left Malaya late in 1951, a very sick and overworked man suffering from the effects of various jungle ailments. He was succeeded by Lieutenant-Colonel John Sloane of the Argyll and Sutherland Highlanders, who, although he had no Special Force or jungle experience, did a fine job in welding the Malayan Scouts into a first-class fighting force.

The early jungle patrols by the Malayan Scouts appeared to validate the concept. One of the Scouts' patrols spent 103 days in the jungle when 7 days was considered a long time for British soldiers to spend on patrol. Apart from achieving some CT eliminations in 1951, the Scouts also took help to local communities, carrying penicillin and simple medicines to Sakai villages and dispensing medical help to the tribespeople. These activities were to be of enormous value in winning over the aborigines. The Scouts' main task, however, was to send out patrols of three or four men from their jungle bases and ambush tracks used by terrorists, a skill which was developed to a fine art in future SAS operations in Malaya and which was to lay the foundation for SAS anti-terrorist tactics elsewhere in the troubled years to come.

Between June and August 1951 the main area of operations was in north-west Johore and Negri Sembilan, where Operations WARBLER, GRASSHOPPER and SEDGE were mounted to make the areas secure and drive the terrorists northwards. Towards the end of 1951 twelve terrorists were killed in the Bentong area of south-west Pahang during Operation MAHAKAL, and in addition seven members of the 24th and 30th Companies, No 6 Regiment MRLA, were killed during Operation PURSUIT, which was mounted after the murder of the High Commissioner, Sir Henry Gurney, near Raub on 6 October.

Also in 1951, a concerted effort was made against elements of No 5 Regiment MRLA in the Tapah and Ipoh areas of southern and central Perak. The first operation there, GALLOWS, was mounted in January, and was followed by a series of others throughout the remainder of the year: RUMBLE, RAINBOW, REDSKIN, RAVEN, ROVER, MERMAID and MARKER between February and August, and SLUDGE, REBEL and SPRINGTIDE from August to December. This whole series of operations resulted in the killing of 14 terrorists, the capture of 33 and the surrender of 4, as well as the destruction of 38 CT camps and the serious disruption of their supply organization.

During these operations, much use was made of Dayak trackers brought in from Borneo. The first Dayaks had arrived in Malaya in 1948, early in the Emergency, to operate with Ferret Force teams, and the number employed had increased steadily ever since. Their tracking skills were of inestimable value in locating CT trails and camps. Several hundred Dayaks in all were brought to Malaya, and eventually formed into a unit known as the Sarawak Rangers.

Terrorist casualties in 1951 were the highest so far in the campaign, with 1,077 killed, 121 captured and a further 201 surrendered, but they succeeded in inflicting substantial casualties on the Security Forces and the civilian population. During the year the Security Forces lost 504 killed and 691 wounded. In one of the worst single incidents, in October 1951, CTs ambushed a patrol of the 1st Battalion, The Queen's Own Royal West Kent Regiment, and killed eleven soldiers for the loss of only six of their own number.

On the civilian side, the death toll in 1951 was 533, with 356 wounded and 135 missing. The main CT targets were still the rubber estates and their staffs, from managers down to tappers; they slashed thousands of trees, burned down factories, attacked the homes of managers and labourers. The Communists showed little restraint or humanity in their campaign now, raiding villages and often treating selected individuals with great savagery. In at least one instance, they nailed a man to a tree through his hands and slowly sliced the flesh from his body, finally cutting his throat.

The CTs extended their murderous attacks for the first time to the wives and children of British planters. In one attack that summer, they shot 2-year-old Susan Thompson, a planter's daughter, through the head while she was riding in the estate Land Rover with the cook, and shortly afterwards they killed Mary Burne, a tin miner's wife, in an ambush on the Taiping–Selama road north of Ipoh. Their car was held up by a log barricade and surrounded by CTs armed with Sten guns. Burne got out, but the terrorists ignored him and opened up on his wife, who was sitting in the front seat. These tactics were deliberately aimed at driving the British planters and miners out of Malaya, on the basis that when a man himself was threatened he might stand and fight, but when his family became the main target he would pack up and leave. Some did, but most remained. The Communists had seriously misinterpreted how the British would react under a threat of this nature.

The real turning point in the anti-terrorist campaign came in October 1951, with the murder of the High Commissioner, Sir Henry Gurney. Although this act was almost certainly not pre-planned, it sent a wave of shock and fear throughout the Federation. If, after three years of anti-terrorist warfare, the MRLA was still effective enough to assassinate the Crown's representative in broad daylight, then the authorities must surely have underestimated the strength and effectiveness of the Communist insurrection.

That was also the view of the new Conservative Government headed by Winston Churchill, which came to office on 21 October 1951. Apart from the near-bankrupt state of the British economy – incredibly, food stocks were lower in 1951 than they had been in the darkest days of the Second World War, ten years earlier – Churchill faced crises everywhere, from the Middle East to Korea. All of them were draining the manpower resources of HM Forces, and yet Churchill's shrewd instinct grasped the fact that if Malaya fell under Communist domination, the rest of Asia would quickly follow. He realized that the war in Malaya was a conflict not only at the crossroads of history, but at the crossroads of Asia. His immediate action, as we have seen, was to despatch his Colonial Secretary, Oliver Lyttelton, to Malaya to make a first-hand assessment of what might be done to remedy what appeared to be a failing situation. His next move was to ensure that the next High Commissioner of the Federation of Malaya would also direct military operations. There would be no more half-hearted measures resulting from a restriction on military power; from now on, the campaign in Malaya would be waged on an unprecedented scale, with more troops and police committed to the theatre.

All this was very necessary, because the MRLA remained a highly effective fighting force. It was also beginning to change its tactics, because the Communists were beginning to realize that their campaign of terror was rapidly alienating the very people they were seeking to 'liberate'.

In October 1951, Chin Peng, the Secretary-General of the MCP, presided over a meeting of the Politburo to work out future policy. The meeting was attended by an unspecified number of officers of the Chinese People's Liberation Army who had infiltrated into Malaya, possibly by sea from Hainan Island. They brought with them their own experiences of discipline, training and, more importantly, tactics and strategy. By all accounts they were not impressed by the MCP and did not stay long in Malaya.

Nevertheless, they probably had an influence on the MCP's future policy, which was set out in a document called the October Directive. Its main theme involved the avoidance of what it termed 'inconvenience' in order to try and win the support of the masses. In practical terms, this meant that identity and ration cards would no longer be seized, there would be no more burning of New Villages or attacks on labourers, post offices, reservoirs, power stations or any public services. Civilian trains would no longer be derailed with high explosives, and great care was to be exercised when throwing grenades or when 'shooting running dogs found mixing with the masses to avoid stray shots hurting the masses'. British officers engaged in health work were not to be molested. However, there were to be no restraints imposed on attacks on the Security Forces, or on the managers of plantations, tin mines and other production centres.

The October Directive was tantamount to an admission that the MCP's strategy in Malaya so far had been a failure. It placed more emphasis on cultivating the support of the masses by legal means, and on attempting to infiltrate the Malayan Federation's political and administrative system while continuing to prosecute a guerrilla campaign from the sanctuary of the jungle. Equal emphasis was to be placed on both strategems. This dual policy of fighting a war of Communist 'liberation' had long been practised by Mao Zedong in China, and it was one that Chin Peng now accepted through the default of his Party's earlier tactics. The unfortunate thing about the October Directive was that it was about a year before a copy of it fell into the hands of the Security Forces.

As far as the MRLA itself was concerned, rigid adherence to the Communist system proved a double-edged sword. On the one hand it encouraged good discipline and rigid camp routines; on the other, it could seriously interfere with command in the field. Every MRLA region, regiment and unit, down to a six-man section, had its own political officer who was equal, and sometimes senior to, the military commander. He had full authority to countermand the military commander's orders and often did so, to the detriment of whatever operation was in hand.

In the early years of the Emergency, before the activities of the Security Forces turned the terrorists into a nomadic force, the standard of their jungle camps was high. Most camps were sited away from jungle tracks but not too far from contact with the Chinese squatter population, and close to fresh water. Each camp had a parade ground, with a Communist flag flying from a central pole during daylight. Some of the camps, all of which were carefully camouflaged, were extensive in area, with sleeping huts, offices, kitchens and stores. They were guarded at all times by a screen of sentries, spaced out in the jungle at a radius of at least 600 yards to cover possible approach routes. Surprise attacks on the camps were rare, but if one materialized the terrorists could make a rapid exit via one of several pre-planned escape routes.

Boredom was the terrorists' worst enemy, and to alleviate it the day was divided into routine activities, beginning with a roll-call at first light. This would be followed by several hours of drill and weapon training, with an hour's break for breakfast at about 09.00. The afternoon would be taken up with camp chores and basic guerrilla warfare tactics until about 17.30, when the CTs would have their evening meal. This was usually followed by about two hours of political instruction, during which terrorists – including officers – were encouraged to stand up and be self-critical. Many terrorists were of low mentality, and this aspect of camp life was very important in their indoctrination; for the first time in their lives, it made them feel that they were an integral part of an enormous organization that spanned the world, and that they had a definite role to play in its eventual triumph.

Great attention was paid to personal hygiene and to the cleanliness of the camp in general, essential in a wet, humid, jungle environment where disease was an ever-present menace and where medical supplies were often in short supply, and perhaps even non-existent. Attempts to turn the MRLA into a fully-uniformed force, to foster the impression that it was a trained army and to boost morale, also met with some success; by the end of 1951 most CTs wore uniforms of khaki or jungle-green, provided by the Min Yuen, with rubber boots, short puttees and a cap bearing the Communist star. Trained fighters at first received a small monthly pay with which they could buy tobacco, soap and other luxuries, but this ceased to be a regular incentive as time wore on.

6

GROUND OPERATIONS PHASE THREE: JANUARY 1952 TO MAY 1954

General Sir Rob Lockhart, who took over as Director of Operations Malaya upon the departure of Lieutenant-General Sir Harold Briggs in December 1951, was determined that there should be no lull in the offensive against the terrorists during the uncertain period before Sir Henry Gurney's successor arrived in the theatre. The deployment of Security Forces in threatened areas continued, and in specific areas search-and-destroy and food denial operations were stepped up.

In January 1952, Operation BRODERICK was launched against the 39th Independent Platoon of No 5 Regiment MRLA in the Kroh Chikus Forest Reserve area of south Perak, while Operation TECHCHI was mounted in the Triang area of south-west Pahang. At least ten terrorists were eliminated during these operations, but occasional stiff firefights, particularly against the experienced No 5 Regiment MRLA, inflicted substantial casualties on the Security Forces. The 1st Battalion The Gordon Highlanders, for example, lost seven men in a carefully planned terrorist ambush while on patrol in January. Further search-and-destroy operations, in February 1952, were PUMA, in the Cameron Highlands area of north-west Pahang, and NOAH in the south-western part of the state.

Outside these main operational areas, Operation PANCAKE was mounted against the 5th Platoon, No 8 Regiment MRLA in Kedah, and Operation HELSBY was launched against the Headquarters of No 12 Regiment MRLA in the Belum Valley area of northern Perak in February. Both these operations were aimed at eliminating ranking members of the MRLA, and were also designed to drive the terrorists away from key food-producing areas.

Operation HELSBY, close to the Thai border, was a combined operation involving three squadrons of the 22nd Special Air Service Regiment, 42 Commando Royal Marines, Gurkha troops and Federation Police. It involved the use of paratroops for the first time in the Malayan campaign, the idea being to drop B Squadron of 22nd SAS to form a blocking party, so preventing the CTs from escaping the main drive by the remainder of the force along the valley.

The idea of using paratroops in operations against the CTs had first been proposed by two former wartime SAS officers, John Cooper and Alastair MacGregor, both of whom had joined the Malayan Scouts. They carried out a series of experimental jumps into the jungle canopy, lowering themselves to the ground on 100-foot ropes, and proved that the technique, although risky, was feasible. The idea was pursued enthusiastically by the second in command of the Scouts (22nd SAS Regiment from 1952), Major Hugh Mercer, and by the beginning of February fifty-four men of B Squadron had been trained accordingly.

The dropping zone in Operation HELSBY consisted of a paddy, easily identifiable from the air, which lay between two jungle-covered massifs rising to 4,000 feet. High ground to the north, however, meant that the four Dakota transport aircraft employed on the operation had to make a tight circuit, followed by a sharp descent to the dropping height and then an immediate sharp climbing turn to port to pull out of the valley. When the aircraft arrived over the dropping zone there was a strengthening east wind, accentuated by the venturi effect of the funnel-shaped valley. The descent by the first man out, known as the 'drifter', showed the strength and direction of the wind, but there was little margin for manoeuvring because one side of the dropping zone was bounded by a fast-flowing river. The 54 paratroops made their exits in sticks of three and all but four men overshot the dropping zone, 44 of them landing in trees up to 150 feet in height. Nevertheless, they sustained only light casualties and were able to concentrate rapidly for their attack on the terrorist target.

From the point of view of terrorist eliminations, Operation HELSBY proved abortive. The foot patrols reached the valley after five days of exhausting marching, moving for up to ten hours a day with only occasional brief halts over mountainous jungle tracks and then dried-up river beds where the sun's heat caused considerable discomfort after the damp of the jungle. They reached the valley only to find that the CTs had decamped, alerted by agents in the villages along the approach route and also by the presence of aircraft. The Security Forces destroyed the terrorists' cultivation plots and withdrew.

Meanwhile, more Commonwealth battalions were arriving for service in Malaya. In January, the Security Forces were joined by the 1st Battalion The Fiji Infantry Regiment and the 1st (Nyasaland) and the 3rd (Kenya) Battalions of The King's African Rifles. Later in the year, the widely scattered independent infantry brigades were grouped into two divisions, the 17th (Gurkha) Division in the north and the 1st Federal Division in the south.

Many of the British Army battalions serving in Malaya in 1952 were virtually National Service battalions. The majority of subalterns were National Service officers, and in some battalions 90 per cent of lance-corporals and 50 per cent of corporals were National Servicemen. About 60 per cent of the private soldiers were conscripts. National Service troops had been used in Malaya since the beginning of the Emergency, and in the early days they had often been thrown in at the deep end. They had little or no jungle experience and even less idea of how to deal with potentially hazardous situations in a terrorist environment. Fears about using conscripts in jungle warfare appeared to be confirmed in the early months of the campaign, when a patrol of the 2nd Battalion The Scots Guards, most of them National Servicemen, shot dead twenty-six Chinese male terrorist suspects in a settlement at Batang Kali, near Kuala Lumpur. The official story was that the Chinese had been shot while trying to escape, but the fact that all were killed and none wounded was in itself suspicious, and the circumstances in which the shooting took place are still unclear.

By 1952, however, the image of the National Serviceman in Malaya had changed completely. Infantry patrols were normally led by a National Service subaltern, backed up by an experienced Regular sergeant and at least one other NCO who was experienced in jungle warfare. Many of the young subalterns became superb leaders, despite their early misgivings over how they might cope in a combat situation against an elusive and cunning enemy; much of their success was attributable to the excellent training they received at the Far East Land Forces School of Jungle Warfare in Johore, where most of the instructors were tough and experienced Australians who had fought in New Guinea against a far deadlier foe than the Communist terrorists. The men, too, quickly adapted themselves to 'jungle bashing'.

Many never saw a terrorist, unless he was a prisoner, but, for those who did, combat in the jungle was a brutal awakening to reality. As one young officer involved in a firefight said later,

> 'I was badly shaken . . . I was awake, gasping with shock. This was real. This was happening. We were shooting people. We were killing them. At first I had been living from second to second, automatically, but now I was awake. We had worked for this for months. This was raw savage success. It was butchery. It was horror.'

But, like seasoned jungle veterans, they became accustomed to it. They coped, and coped very well, and boys of 19 emerged from the jungle as men with leadership experience that would carry them through any experience they might encounter on their return to civilian life.

In April 1952 a further operation, LEAGUE, was mounted against the CTs in the Cameron Highlands, followed by Operation HIVE in the Sermban area of north-west Negri Sembilan in the summer. During this operation a patrol of the 1st Battalion The Green Howards achieved a noteworthy success when, acting on intelligence provided by a surrendered Min Yuen leader named Nam Fook, they located a terrorist camp near Tampin. The patrol commander, Captain Bagnall (later General Sir Nigel Bagnall, KCB, CVO, MC), carried out a detailed reconnaissance and moved his platoon to the perimeter of the CT camp under cover of darkness, launching a devastating attack at dawn and killing seven terrorists. The Green Howards had a very successful three-year tour in Malaya; by the time they left in October 1952 they had accounted for 103 terrorists for the loss of one officer and eight men killed in action.

The most successful British battalion, however, was the 1st Battalion The Suffolk Regiment. They spent two and a half years in Malaya, and by the time their tour ended in January 1953 they had eliminated 195 terrorists for a loss of 12 killed and 24 wounded. Their most important single achievement came during operations in July 1952, when they killed a notorious CT leader named Liew Kon Kim – also known as the Bearded Terror of Kajang – in the Kuala Langat swamp 15 miles from Kajang. Special Branch had received intelligence of Liew Kon Kim's whereabouts from a Min Yuen defector, and had called in the Suffolks to mount a sweep of the suspect area, backed up by two companies of the Royal West Kent Regiment. The task of combing the area of the swamp where the CT leader was said to be hiding was assigned to B Company of the Suffolks commanded by Major Malcolm Dewar, and after six days of patrolling their perseverence was rewarded.

At 14.30 on 6 July, 2nd Lieutenant Raymond Hands and two men, Privates K. Baker and W. Wynant – all National Servicemen – were scouting ahead of their platoon when they were guided to what proved to be the CT camp by the sound of a radio. They came on a hut in the swamp and opened fire; three CTs – including a woman who was Liew Kon Kim's mistress – fled, but Hands killed all three with his Patchet gun. The terrorist leader had been responsible for many savage assaults on plantations, and his elimination was a notable coup for which Hands was awarded the MC.

Several other Communist leaders were also eliminated in 1952. In May, the commander of the 10th (Malay) Regiment MRLA was killed by a Gurkha patrol as he was walking down a jungle trail on the edge of a rubber estate near Kuantan in east Pahang. Another CT commander, 'Shorty' Kuk, a member of the Central Committee of the MCP, was beheaded by his own bodyguards, who brought his head along with them when they gave themselves up and claimed the reward of $200,000.

Other CT leaders surrendered; they included Moo Tay Mei, a prominent regional political officer who claimed to have become disillusioned with Communism, and Ming Lee, another high-ranking CT. He had remained an elusive target for a long time and had eluded the most recent attempts to capture him by the Special Branch and the 1st Battalion The South Wales Borderers; then he simply walked out of the jungle and gave himself up, with the astonishing statement, for someone who had been a dedicated CT, that the Communists were no longer any good and that the Security Forces were winning anyway.

There was no doubt that in 1952, under the energetic leadership of General Templer, the Security Forces *were* winning. In April 1952, 107 CTs were killed, and in June the number rose to 109, the highest ever monthly total. The number of terrorists killed in the course of the year was 1,148, the highest figure of the entire Emergency; 123 were captured and 256 surrendered. The Security Forces lost 263 killed and 401 wounded, about half the previous year's casualty total, while civilian casualties showed a marked decline too, with 343 killed, 158 wounded and 131 missing.

The military plan for 1953 envisaged a series of major offensives against the MRLA regiments in the central states of Malacca, Pahang, Negri Sembilan and Selangor, where they were weakest. The aim was to drive a wedge between the main terrorist forces in the north and south of the country, establishing 'White Areas' which would then be held securely by the Federation Police and the Home Guard, while the bulk of the Army was freed to deal with stronger terrorist concentrations in Johore and Perak.

Between January and June 1953, Operations SCREW, COMMODORE and CORNWALL were mounted against Nos 3 and 4 Regiments MRLA, principally in the Kluang and Segamat areas of northern Johore. The task of the Security Forces involved in Operation COMMODORE, which began on 24 May, was to try and capture the State Committee of the MCP. Fifteen SAS paratroops were successfully dropped into deep jungle to form a blocking party, while the main force of 564 troops was airlifted into the operational area by helicopter. During the two-week operation, nine terrorists were killed and fourteen of their camps destroyed.

Some of these operations in Johore were characterized by short but vicious firefights. On 8 April, during Operation SCREW, a ten-man patrol of the 1st Battalion The Cameronians led by 2nd Lieutenant Ian Wightwick (another National Service officer) was carrying out a jungle sweep in the Labis area when contact was made with a CT camp in dense, swampy, secondary jungle. Wightwick formed his men into an extended line with the Bren section on the right flank and launched his attack, killing a CT machine-gunner. Although wounded twice, Wightwick continued to direct the action, which lasted twenty minutes, and in that time he refused to have his wounds dressed. The citation that accompanied the subsequent award of his Military Cross stated:

> The pain from the wounds must have been intense yet 2nd Lieutenant Wightwick at no time gave in to it and it was due to his outstanding leadership and example that this battle was brought to a successful conclusion. Three enemy bodies were recovered, many more were seen to be wounded and doubtless some of them died in the jungle. A large quantity of weapons, equipment and supplies were recovered . . . .

Between March and July 1953, Operations CATO, MATADOR and SWORD were launched against No 6 Regiment MRLA in the Raub, Mentakab and Bentong areas of south-west Pahang and the Bongsu Forest Reserve area of southern Kedah. Operation SWORD, which lasted into 1954, was very successful, the units involved killing 36 CTs, capturing 19 and destroying 106 camps. Two infantry battalions were almost continuously employed in the operation. One was the 2nd/10th Gurkha Rifles, one of whose soldiers carried out a very gallant act that brought him the award of the Distinguished Conduct Medal. He was Rifleman Narparsad Limbu, one of a patrol of four men who came upon a strongly fortified enemy camp, complete with bunker positions and thirty CTs who were ready to stand and fight. The patrol commander was killed and two men wounded, but Narparsad continued fighting until all his ammunition was exhausted. He collected more from the dead man and his wounded colleague and, single-handed, forced the CTs to retreat. He then hid the body of his patrol commander, dressed the wounds of one of the wounded men and then, having left him food and water, hid him in the jungle. (The other wounded man had fallen down a gully during the action and was not found until the following day). After nightfall, Narparsad collected all the patrol's weapons and made his way back to his platoon's base camp, which he reached at dawn after a stiff climb. He then led a patrol back to the scene of the action and recovered the wounded and the body of the patrol commander.

Operations WELLINGTON II and MAZE were mounted against No 1 Regiment MRLA in the Port Swettenham and Kuala Lumpur districts of Selangor between April and December 1953, while Operation IBEX was directed against No 7 Regiment MRLA in the Kuantan area of east Pahang during August. Four infantry battalions were assigned to Operation VALIANT, which was mounted in the deep jungle of north-west Pahang from October to December 1953 against the ever-troublesome No 5 Regiment MRLA and, in particular, against the Central Politburo of the MCP, which intelligence had indicated was in the area. Unfortunately, the Politburo – some eighty strong, including its escort –

eluded the Security Forces and slipped across the border into Thailand, where it remained for the duration of the Emergency.

In the course of 1953, the Security Forces killed 947 terrorists and captured 73; 372 more surrendered, the highest figure of the Emergency. The Security Forces lost 92 killed and 117 wounded, while civilian casualties amounted to 85 killed, 15 wounded and 43 missing. The reduction in friendly forces' and civilian casualties was dramatic, and a further indication that the terrorists were being beaten. In October 1953, General Templer announced the establishment of the first 'White Area', the prosperous coastal strip of Malacca, and Emergency restrictions there were lifted.

Also by the end of 1953, for the first time, the majority of the infantry battalions engaged in anti-terrorist operations were Malayan. There were now eight Malayan battalions, seven British, seven Gurkha, one African and one Fijian. The Malayan battalions were now efficient and well-trained, and would continue to play an increasing part in the campaign.

The successes of the Security Forces in 1953 provided an enormous boost for public morale. The growing feeling that the forces of law and order had the situation under control was fostered by a series of public relations operations which were designed to improve the public's attitude towards the police and the Emergency Regulations that were still in force in most areas, as well as to encourage the public to provide information on terrorist movements. Much attention was also devoted to depriving the terrorists of the support of the local aboriginal population, and the number of forts in the deep-jungle areas of Perak, Pahang and Kelantan was increased to seven during the year.

On 30 May 1954, General Templer handed over his duties to the new High Commissioner, Sir Donald MacGillivray, and left Malaya. Lieutenant-General Sir Geoffrey Bourne assumed the post of Director of Operations.

Templer had achieved much during his tenure. The fact that he had suffered so few reverses, either political or military, during his time in office must be attributed to his wisdom and leadership, to his resolution and boundless energy. He had shown leadership of a quality which the Communists could not hope to match. Yet he departed with a warning. The Emergency was far from over, and there were still tough times ahead.

7

THE BEGINNING OF THE END

Military operations in Malaya during 1954 followed the pattern of the previous year, being concentrated in the central states of Malaya in order to isolate the main bodies of terrorists in southern Johore and northern Perak. The biggest effort was mounted against No 5 Regiment MRLA in the Ipoh and Sungei Siput areas of southern Perak. Three operations, GALWAY, INLAND and TERMITE were carried out in these areas.

Operation TERMITE was the biggest combined operation mounted so far during the Emergency, and began with a drop of 180 paratroops of A, B and D Squadrons of the 22nd Special Air Service Regiment into the Kinta and Raia valleys east of Ipoh. The paratroops used a modified version of abseiling gear that had first been tried out operationally in July 1953, when fifty men of 22nd SAS had been dropped into the Bongsu Forest Reserve area of south Kedah during Operation SWORD. The abseiling equipment consisted of 200 feet of webbing carried in a bag attached to a special harness, and replaced the earlier knotted rope which the SAS paratroopers had used to descend from the treetops – a very fatiguing process. During the drop in Operation SWORD the SAS had suffered three fatalities when the abseil harness attachment failed. The modified version, perfected by the Parachute Training School, worked well, and the forty paratroops who needed to use the equipment during TERMITE suffered only seven minor injuries, a casualty rate that compared favourably with paratrooping operations over open country.

Having landed on dropping zones previously marked with smoke candles by an Auster aircraft of No 656 Squadron, the paratroops cut dropping zones into which heavy supplies were dropped by re-supply aircraft. These included mechanical saws and explosives for the preparation of helicopter pads. Although Operation TERMITE produced the disappointing total of only fifteen terrorist eliminations, it completely validated the use of paratroops in combined operations of this kind. Plans were accordingly laid for establishing a fourth squadron of 22nd SAS Regiment and for training four more paratroop companies, one Malay and three Gurkha. Standing orders were also prepared for reinforcing jungle forts by paratroops in case of emergency.

However, few opportunities occurred after 1954 for major paratrooping operations, as it was soon established that forces without special training in airborne operations could be airlifted into the jungle more rapidly, and with much less personal risk, by helicopter. When paratroops were used on combined operations, it was usually to prepare landing pads for helicopters in the jungle. On some occasions, helicopters were themselves used to drop paratroops when an accurate drop into a target area was needed; the helicopter's ability to hover at about 750 feet above ground level, the absence of slipstream and its double exit made it a very suitable vehicle for this type of operation.

Other operations mounted during 1954 included HAWK and APOLLO against No 6 Regiment MRLA in the Raub and Kuala Lipis areas of Pahang, JEKYLL against No 2 Regiment MRLA in the Bahau area of Negri Sembilan and KITCHENER and AJAX against No 4 Regiment MRLA in the Rangam and Kulai areas of Johore. Two hundred and forty-three terrorists were eliminated during these operations and a high proportion of the eliminations involved surrendered CTs, a sure indication that the morale of the MRLA was continuing to crack in the face of a continuing and determined Security Forces offensive.

Combined operations during 1954 also led to the establishment of more 'White Areas'. In January the coastal area of Trengganu was declared 'White', followed by parts of Perlis and Kedah in February, and parts of Negri Sembilan in March. The inhabitants of these areas, now freed of restrictions, were warned that the Communists might try to infiltrate in search of food; if this happened, the police were to be informed immediately. It did happen, in Malacca, in March 1954, with the result that four CTs were killed by Security Forces acting on information received. It seemed that the people were by no means anxious to return to life under the Emergency Regulations; never once during the remainder of the Emergency was the Government forced to reimpose controls on a 'White Area'.

By the middle of 1954 the average number of civilian and military personnel killed each month was 35, in contrast to 188 during the terrible year of 1951. Since the start of the Emergency over 7,500 terrorists had been eliminated, and only 3,500 still remained at large in the jungle. These, however, represented the hard core of the MRLA, and the nature of the terrain in the jungle-clad spinal range to which they had retreated ensured that they were becoming increasingly difficult to locate and that they could not be entirely prevented from attacking targets close to the jungle, especially in areas where pressure by the Security Forces had been relaxed. It was also clear, by the early summer of 1954, that the terrorist leaders were inflicting harsh disciplinary measures on their rank and file in order to discourage them from defecting, and were also undertaking more aggressive action against selected targets in an attempt to raise morale.

During the whole of 1954 the terrorists lost 709 killed and 51 captured; 211 more surrendered. The Security Forces casualties were 87 killed and 154 wounded, while civilian casualties amounted to 97 killed, 31 wounded and 57 missing. By the beginning of 1955 nearly one-third of the population of Malaya was living in 'White Areas', and throughout the year the terrorists followed a policy of avoiding contact with the Security Forces whenever possible.

The main area of operations in 1955 was Pahang, where the Security Forces launched a major offensive against No 6 Regiment MRLA and its supporting Min Yuen cell. Lieutenant-General Sir Geoffrey Bourne's strategy was first of all to drive the terrorists from Pahang, then continue operations in neighbouring Negri Sembilan and Selangor in order to create a complete 'White Area' across central Malaya from Malacca to the east coast, at the same time severing the main courier routes between the Northern Bureau of the MCP, now in refuge in the Bentong salient of southern Thailand, and the Southern Bureau of the MCP in Johore. Operation SHARK, which had been launched in September 1954, also continued throughout 1955 against the 26th Independent Platoon MRLA in the Sungei Siput area of Perak, and achieved thirty-five terrorist eliminations by the end of the year.

Operations in Pahang during 1955 were ROOSTER in the Kuala Lipis area, HUNTSMAN in the Raub area and LATIMER NORTH, LATIMER SOUTH and ASP in the Temerloh and Triang areas. Most of these operations had been designed to last for a maximum of sixth months; in fact some of them, notably the LATIMER series which began late in 1955, were to last for two years or more as the Security Forces maintained their pressure on the enemy.

From February 1955, Security Forces operations in Malaya were aided by a working agreement with Thailand. As part of this, a joint Malay–Thai Intelligence Centre was established at Songkhla, just over the Thai border, and a frontier planning staff formed. A border agreement between the two countries had already existed for some time, permitting anti-terrorist security patrols to operate up to 20 miles inside each other's territory, and this had proved a valuable arrangement; in 1954 Federation Police had harassed CTs over the border, causing much disruption. The agreement was now extended to allow British aircraft and helicopters to operate on the Thai side of the border.

In July 1955 there came a positive move towards preparing Malaya for self-government, when a general election was held and Tunku Abdul Rahman, the leader of the UMNO, formed a government known as the Triple Alliance, which was a coalition of the UMNO, the Malayan

Chinese Association (MCA) and the Malayan Indian Congress. One of Tunku Abdul Rahman's first acts was to proclaim an amnesty, initially without a time limit, enabling terrorists to surrender and receive free pardons, the exceptions being those who were known to have carried out criminal acts. Security Forces operations were halted, and millions of leaflets explaining the terms of the amnesty were air-dropped and otherwise distributed.

The results of the amnesty, however, were extremely disappointing. By the end of November 1955 only thirty terrorists had surrendered – possibly because of strict security measures in the CT jungle camps which made it virtually impossible for anyone to slip away – and in the meantime there had been a number of terrorist incidents, culminating in an attack on a village in the Cameron Highlands on 21 November.

In the autumn of 1955 there were twenty-two infantry battalions in Malaya, divided between seven brigades: the 1st and 2nd Federal Infantry, the 18th Independent Infantry, the 26th, 63rd and 99th Gurkha Infantry and the 28th Commonwealth Infantry. The latter, comprising British and Australian battalions, an Australian artillery battery and a New Zealand engineer squadron, was the last to be formed, in October 1955.

When it was clear that the amnesty offered to the Communists was not working, offensive operations by the Security Forces resumed, although now personnel were required to challenge terrorists and ask them to surrender before opening fire. From the Security Forces' point of view it was an unsatisfactory and often highly dangerous position to be in, as Sergeant Ramsor Rai of the 1st/6th Gurkha Rifles discovered one day late in 1955 when, with one other Gurkha, he came upon an occupied camp with ten insurgents. He sent his man back for reinforcements and continued to observe the terrorist camp from a distance of 20 yards. The reinforcements arrived in due course; they consisted of one man, a machine-gunner, the rest of Rai's company having gone off on another operation in the meantime. Despite the odds against him Ramsor stood up and called upon the CTs to surrender. Their response was to open fire and run away. Ramsor killed three of them, and if it had not been for the need to comply with the amnesty orders he would almost certainly have killed the lot. He was awarded the DCM for this action.

In August 1955 the 1st/10th Gurkhas became the first and only battalion in Malaya to kill 300 terrorists. The record of all the Gurkha battalions during the Emergency was exemplary, and they achieved more in terms of CT eliminations than any other force engaged in the long and difficult campaign.

The Security Forces' offensive continued in December 1955 with Operations LATIMER NORTH and LATIMER SOUTH. These were mainly food denial operations, and by the end of the year, following earlier operations, they had resulted in the decimation of No 6 Regiment MRLA and the disintegration of the local Communist Terrorist Organization and its supporting Min Yuen cell. Over 130 terrorists were eliminated, one of the three deep-jungle bases which the terrorists had been trying to establish was destroyed and the whole of Pahang was cleared of terrorists with the exception of the Temerloh and Cameron Highlands areas.

At the end of 1955, a meeting took place between Tunku Abdul Rahman and Chin Peng, the Secretary-General of the Malayan Communist Party. The meeting had its origin in a letter from Chin Peng addressed to the Tunku in September, in which he said that the MCP was willing to send an emissary to negotiate peace and discuss an amnesty. A preliminary meeting was held between Government and MCP representatives at the village of Klian Intan, a few miles from the Thai border, on 17 November, and this paved the way for the big meeting between the two leaders. On 22 December, the Security Forces were ordered to observe a ceasefire for ten days in a 400-square-mile area in northern Perak and Kedah, centred on the village of Baling, about 20 miles from the Thai frontier, where the rendezvous was to take place.

The meeting was held over a two-day period on 28 and 29 December 1955 and was abortive. Tunku Abdul Rahman insisted on the dissolution of the MCP, and on subsequent proof through investigation that its members would be loyal to Malaya. The terms were generous enough; any surrendered terrorists would be freed after a period of detention or, if they wished, repatriated to China. After lengthy negotiation Chin Peng agreed to the disbandment of the MRLA, but insisted that the MCP must be recognized as a legal political party after Malaya achieved full independence.

It was a standpoint that was clearly unacceptable to the Tunku, who made it clear that one side was going to have to give in, and that it would not be the Government. Chin Peng countered by saying that if the Government demanded the total surrender of the Communists, they would prefer to fight to the last man. So the talks broke down; Chin Peng returned to the jungle, and on 8 February 1956 the amnesty came to an end.

The Communist failure to produce any tangible result from the peace talks resulted in a considerable loss of face for Chin Peng and the Politburo. They had lost the shooting war; all they could do now was play for time and attempt to regain some of the popular support for their cause, which was now swiftly evaporating. The pretext that they were fighting to liberate Malaya and its peoples from Imperialist domination no longer held water; at a conference held in London between 18 January and 8 February 1956, it was announced that 'a constitution providing for full independence and self-government for Malaya would be introduced at the earliest possible date'.

The MCP's only hope now was to remain intact until such time as it could leave the jungle under some form of guarantee that it would be allowed to remain in existence, and to this end Chin Peng and his colleagues launched a 'peace offensive' early in 1956 in an attempt to lay the blame for the continuing Emergency on the Federal Government. The message that Chin Peng now sought to get across to the Chinese element of the populace was that the eyes of the world were now on the plight of the MCP, and that the latter was prepared to hold out until it received external Communist aid to continue the fight or until a further opportunity presented itself for renewing a 'popular revolution'.

Although terrorist contacts and incidents declined during 1956 as a result of this 'wait and see' policy, the Security Forces succeeded in eliminating 473 CTs in the course of the year, which represented 20 per cent of their remaining strength. At the end of 1956 the number of CTs still at large in the jungle was estimated to be 2,063.

One of the Security Forces' biggest coups occurred in April 1956, with the elimination of Yeong Kwo, the Deputy Secretary-General of the MCP. For some time he had been known to be operating in the Kuala Lumpur area; then, in March 1956, a tapper came in with the information that he had seen a suspicious Chinese camping in a rubber estate near Semenyih, in south Selangor. Special Branch officers set about tracking down the suspect and called in patrols of the 1st Battalion The Rifle Brigade, and one of these, led by Lieutenant Robin Alers-Hankey, succeeded in killing Yeong Kwo, who had been mainly responsible for the MCP's political offensive. Among his possessions Special Branch officers found comprehensive documentation on the MCP's plans to subjugate Malaya by subversion.

The most important operations carried out by the Security Forces in 1956 were SHARK NORTH and SHARK SOUTH in the Ipoh, Sungei Siput and Cameron Highlands areas of Perak, GABES NORTH and GABES SOUTH in the Kelantan and Perak border areas, BONANZA in southern Selangor, LATIMER SOUTH and ENTER in the Bahau and Rompin areas of north and north-east Negri Sembilan and HUCKSTER and TARTAN ROCK in the Kluang and Kulai areas of Johore. LATIMER SOUTH and ENTER were mounted against the South Malayan Bureau of the MCP and employed considerable helicopter support, as did HUCKSTER and BONANZA. These operations resulted in the elimination of over 150 terrorists during the year.

Paratrooping operations by the 22nd Special Air Service Regiment were also expanded during 1956, in order to clear landing areas for trooplifting helicopters and also to track down terrorist camps. At this time the SAS in Malaya was undergoing some changes. C Squadron, whose men had not always found it easy to adapt themselves to the 'winning of hearts and minds' aspect of the Regiment's work and whose men had proved to be more susceptible to jungle diseases than those of the other squadrons, returned to Rhodesia. They were replaced by a New Zealand Special Air Service Squadron, whose men had been well trained in SAS techniques at home before flying to Malaya for further training in jungle warfare. They included a number of Maoris, who rapidly became expert trackers. An additional squadron (making five in all, and bringing the Regiment's strength to 560 men) was also attached; this was the Independent Squadron of the Parachute Regiment, commanded by Major Dudley Coventry. The first batch of Fijian soldiers was also attached to the SAS in 1956, proving an excellent asset.

The military strategy during 1956 was to exploit the successes achieved in central Malaya by switching the focus of operations to Selangor and Negri Sembilan, prior to a final offensive against the terrorists in Perak and Johore. By the end of the year a further eight 'White Areas' had been established, containing over a quarter of a million people. More than half the Federation was now 'White'.

On 1 January 1957, military priorities were switched from Negri Sembilan and Selangor, where few terrorist targets remained, to southern Perak and northern Johore. Some 170 terrorist leaders still remained at large in these areas and the CTO was still relatively intact, well-supported by the local Min Yuen. The LATIMER SOUTH operation in Negri Sembilan was taken over by the Federation Police, leaving the Army free to concentrate on Operations SHARK NORTH, SHARK SOUTH and CHIEFTAIN in the Ipoh, Cameron Highlands and Tapah areas of Perak and Operations COBBLE, SHOE and HUCKSTER in the Gemas, Segamat and Kluang areas of Johore.

The overall aim was to create a 'White Area' from Tapah in the north to Kluang in the south before Independence Day, on 31 August 1957, and this was largely achieved. By the end of August the last platoon of the MRLA in Selangor and Negri Sembilan had been eliminated and central Selangor had been declared free of terrorists, completing the 'White' belt extending from coast to coast. In July 1957, for the first time in the Emergency, no military or civilian personnel were killed by terrorist action and there were no major incidents. On Independence Day about 1,830 terrorists were still at large; of these, 500 were in central Perak and 500 in Johore. Some 450 others had sought sanctuary across the Thai border, with only about 100 operating in the jungle on the Malayan side.

8

THE FINAL PHASE

The final phase of the insurgent war in Malaya may be said to have lasted from 31 August 1957, when the country gained complete independence, to July 1960, when the Emergency was formally declared over. During this period Communist terrorism and the hold of the Malayan Communist Party over its remaining adherents declined sharply until, in the end, neither represented a continued threat to the stability of the nation.

In September 1957 terrorist eliminations fell to only fifteen, the lowest monthly total of the Emergency so far, and the total for the whole of the year was only 394. As Independence Day approached the Federal Government came under some pressure to come to terms with the remaining terrorists, but its leaders knew that it would be foolhardy to compromise the position that had been won so arduously, and at such a cost in human life and property, and so it was decided that the Emergency would remain in force for at least a year following Independence. At the same time, it was thought desirable to reduce the number of Commonwealth troops engaged in anti-terrorist operations, to restrict their use as far as possible to southern Johore and northern Perak, and to avoid bringing them into direct contact with the populace.

On 3 September 1957 Tunku Abdul Rahman announced a fresh amnesty, which was to remain in force for four months. Under revised terms, members of the MCP could now be repatriated with their families to China without prior interrogation, should they not be prepared to renounce Communism. Operations by the Security Forces would continue, but special arrangements would be made for insurgents who wished to surrender.

By this time about one-third of the MRLA's active force was in Thailand, their leaders determined to lie dormant until such time as the Malayan Government would be deluded into believing that they no longer represented a threat and would therefore negotiate peace on the MCP's terms. It was an empty belief, and the continuing

Security Forces operations in Malaya underlined the Government's determination to carry on the campaign until the last remnants of the MRLA were eliminated.

The main operational areas during 1958 were central Perak and southern and eastern Johore, with mopping-up operations continuing in Negri Sembilan, southern Pahang, Selangor and southern Perak as a secondary task. In the latter area, Operation CHIEFTAIN, which had begun in 1957, continued until November 1958, by which time only ten terrorists were still at large in the operational area. These were dealt with by the Police Field Force and the area was declared 'White' shortly afterwards.

The most successful operation during this period was BINTANG, which was mounted in central Perak against a hard core of seventy terrorists known to be still at large there. It lasted until September 1958 and was conducted mainly by the 2nd Federal Infantry Brigade, assisted by various Commonwealth units that included Nos 92 and 93 Field Squadrons of the RAF Regiment (Malaya). No 92 Squadron, which came under the command of the 2nd Battalion The Royal Malay Regiment, claimed ten terrorist kills and made a valuable contribution to the operation by constantly patrolling and ambushing courier routes and by destroying food dumps.

When Operation BINTANG ended, sixty-one terrorists had been eliminated and the few that had escaped the Security Forces' net by fleeing north-eastwards to the area between Ipoh and Grik were dealt with by the 3rd Battalion The Royal Malay Regiment in Operation GINGER.

In Selangor, mopping-up operations by the 1st Battalion The Royal Malay Regiment and other units, involving food denial operations carried out in conjunction with systematic shelling by the Army and air strikes by the RAF, led to the surrender of twenty-seven terrorists in one month in the Sekinchang Swamp area. The remainder were flushed out of the Rasa area and either surrendered or fled northwards.

One of the more notable operations of 1958 was carried out in February by D Squadron of the 22nd Special Air Service Regiment, commanded by Major Harry Thompson of the Royal Highland Fusiliers. Their target was a ruthless terrorist called Ah Hoi, who was known to the police as the 'baby killer' because he had once slashed with his knife the pregnant wife of a man he believed to be an informer. The base of Ah Hoi and his group of bandits was in a large coastal swamp area, 18 miles by 10, north of Telok Anson in Selangor, from where they emerged periodically to terrorize the local rubber estates. The continuing threat they presented caused large numbers of Security Forces personnel to be tied down on guard duties around the plantations, and so the SAS was called in to deal with them once and for all.

Major Thompson planned to use two troops of his thirty-seven-strong force to flush out Ah Hoi, holding the other two troops and his small tactical HQ in readiness to attack once the terrorists were located. The two spearhead troops were dropped from a Blackburn Beverley transport aircraft into the jungle canopy near the western edge of the swamp, suffering one serious casualty when the parachute canopy of one trooper collapsed and he landed heavily, breaking his back (he was evacuated by helicopter).

The plan called for D Squadron to patrol eastwards towards the heart of the swamp, which involved wading through rust-brown water and glutinous, stinking mud, infested by leeches and overgrown with mangroves. (The brown stain in the water was caused by iron, and it is interesting to note that because of this, SAS medical staff believed that patrolling through swamp country for lengthy periods actually resulted in less sickness than did normal jungle patrolling.)

The spearhead patrol, led by Captain (later Brigadier) Peter de la Billière, spent ten days moving along the line of the Tengi River, picking up occasional small signs that terrorists had passed that way. Sometimes they waded neck-deep in the marsh channels, at others they swam in open water. At night they slept in hammocks slung between trees, or on improvised rafts if no suitable trees were available. Each man carried enough food for fourteen days, as there was no possibility of being re-supplied by air.

On the eighth day the second troop, led by Sergeant Sandilands, sighted two terrorists and opened fire on them, wounding one. Following the wounded man's trail, they found a CT camp about 4 miles into the swamp and radioed its position, whereupon Major Thompson put the two remaining troops into the swamp from the eastern side. A military and police cordon was also placed around the whole area, this operation taking ten days.

The spearhead SAS patrols had now been in the swamp for three weeks and were reduced to living off the land. Some of the men were in a bad way from exhaustion, the debilitating effects of leeches and ulcerated wounds caused by thorns. Then a frail, sickly girl emerged from the swamp and approached the police cordon with Ah Hoi's offer of surrender; he wanted £3,500 for each of his gang and freedom for those already in prison. She was told to go back to him with the simple message: either surrender within twenty-four hours or be killed in the swamp.

Ah Hoi duly emerged with two CTs. Meanwhile, Major Thompson led a troop after the girl, who had promised to lead them to the remaining terrorists, but she was so exhausted by starvation and disease that she was unable to continue. Thompson therefore held his troop at the edge of the swamp until seven more terrorists surrendered a couple of days later.

In Negri Sembilan, Operation LATIMER SOUTH was halted for most of the year while Police Special Branch officers carried out their own operations in the area. The biggest success of 1958 was in Johore, where 160 terrorists were persuaded to give themselves up following the defection of the former State Committee Member, Hor Lung, who on 5 April 1958, after years of eluding the Security Forces and on one occasion narrowly escaping death in an air attack, calmly walked into the hamlet of Kampong Tengah and surrendered to a policeman.

Hor Lung was promised huge rewards if he would persuade his former colleagues to turn themselves in, and he obliged beyond the wildest dreams of Special Branch. His own surrender had been kept so secret that not a single terrorist knew that it had happened, and when he returned to the jungle on police instructions, visiting each CT branch and committee in turn, they had no reason to disbelieve him when he informed them that, due to a change in policy, armed resistance was to cease. One by one he led the scattered terrorist groups out of the jungle, until after four months of patient work the Malayan Government announced the surrender of 132 rank-and-file terrorists, plus 28 hard-core unit commanders who were put on show to prove it. It was the biggest mass surrender of the Emergency, and for Chin Peng it was a catastrophe of enormous proportions.

All semblance of political and operational control of the terrorists in the southern half of the Federation ceased with the destruction of the South Malaya Bureau of the MCP. The disruption was completed through two more operations: TIGER, which was mounted against the south Johore Regional Committee of the MCP in August 1958, and BADAK, which resulted in the elimination of the 9th Independent Platoon of the MRLA in the eastern part of the state. As a result of these and other smaller-scale operations, the whole of Johore was declared 'White' on 31 December 1958.

At the end of 1958, the number of terrorists still at large had been reduced to 868, including 485 in southern Thailand, 300 in Kedah and north Perak, and several small but fanatical bands in Pahang.

The last series of operations to root out the remaining terrorists began in mid-1959 with Operation SELADANG, which resulted in several eliminations of hard-core CTs in Pahang. After this, the final phase of the military campaign was directed against terrorist bands in the border areas of Kedah and Perak with Thailand.

Operation BROOKLYN was mounted in Kedah in September 1959, while Operation BAMBOO opened in north Perak in October. These operations continued until the official end of the Emergency in July 1960, the Commonwealth forces engaged including the 1st Battalion The Royal Australian Regiment and the 1st Battalion 3rd East Anglian Regiment.

9

OFFENSIVE AIR OPERATIONS

Although the Royal Air Force and associated Commonwealth units concentrated their efforts in support of the Security Forces' activities against the Communist terrorists during the twelve years of the Emergency, their primary role remained the air defence of Malaya, the colony of Singapore, North Borneo and Sarawak.

Air operations in support of the ground forces during Operation FIREDOG came under the overall control of the Commander-in-Chief, Air Command Far East which was redesignated the Far East Air Force on 1 June 1949, the operational control being exercised by the Air Officer Commanding, Malaya.

The onset of the Emergency soon revealed that the RAF was badly placed to mount major anti-terrorist operations, both from the point of view of offensive support and air supply. From a front-line strength of 70 squadrons, with 1,324 operational aircraft, which Air Command South-East Asia had possessed in mid-1945, Air Command Far East's strength had shrunk to 11 squadrons with just over 100 aircraft by the middle of 1948. These limited resources were concentrated entirely on Singapore Island, the mainland air base of Kuala Lumpur having closed down, and so the prospect of setting up a mobile air task on the Malayan peninsula posed considerable problems.

Nevertheless, it was rightly appreciated that control of operational aircraft positioned at forward bases in Malaya could not be effectively exercised from Air HQ at Changi, on Singapore, and so on 6 July 1948 an Advanced Air HQ was set up at Kuala Lumpur, not as part of the task force on the newly re-opened airfield but alongside the Army HQ Malaya District in the town itself. A joint operations and intelligence centre was also set up there, with staff from all three services, the police and the civil service.

This close liaison between all services was to remain a principal characteristic of the anti-terrorist campaign, and centralization of effort became of paramount importance. As far as the Air Forces' commitment was concerned, operations at first were directed both by Rear AHQ at Changi and Advanced AHQ at Kuala Lumpur, the former being responsible for Army support operations in the Johore sub-district and the latter for air operations in central and northern Malaya, but on 1 November 1949 Advanced AHQ was given operational control of all aircraft operating against the terrorists.

Such, broadly, was the structure of the Air Forces in the Malayan theatre during the early months of the Emergency. What they achieved in the years of the anti-terrorist campaign is worth examining in detail, not only because their effort was vital to the eventual outcome of FIREDOG, but because it produced new strides forward in co-operation between air and ground forces, as well as new techniques which were to be refined and developed in later years.

At the beginning of the Malayan Emergency the resources available to HQ Air Command Far East (ACFE) for undertaking offensive operations were very slender, amounting to the equivalent of only three and a half squadrons with twenty-nine aircraft between them. At Sembawang, Nos 28 and 60 Squadrons had sixteen Spitfire FR.18s and PR.19s, while No 84 Squadron at Tengah was equipped with eight Bristol Beaufighters and No 209 Squadron at Seletar had four Short Sunderland flying boats.

On 3 July 1948 three Spitfires of No 60 Squadron flew north to Kuala Lumpur to form the nucleus of an air-strike task force, and were joined shortly afterwards by the remaining aircraft of the squadron together with one photo-reconnaissance PR.19 of No 28 Squadron. On 6 July, two Spitfires of No 60 Squadron armed with cannon and rocket projectiles attacked and virtually destroyed a terrorist camp near Ayer Karah in Perak. The next strike was flown on 15 July, against a group of huts located in mountainous country near Bentong in Pahang, and on the following day another strike was mounted against a hut near Telok Anson in central Perak which was surrounded by swamp and was not easily accessible from the ground. This attack was very successful, ten terrorists being killed.

On 28 July, No 60 Squadron's Spitfires carried out a further air strike in support of a road convoy of the Malay Regiment at Sungei Yu, which had run into an ambush while on its way to relieve a police post at Gua Musang which had been captured by terrorists. Although strike aircraft were kept at a readiness state of four hours during this early period of operations, their reaction time was in fact considerably less, and the speed of the response from Kuala Lumpur was greatly appreciated by the ground forces. The success of the early strikes emphasized the value of fighter-bomber support, and demands for offensive support operations increased sharply in August 1948. The majority of these were carried out in support of SHAWFORCE, the Malay/Gurkha force operating in the Pulai valley of northern Perak.

The Spitfires, however, were showing their age, and when faulty wiring in one of them caused the accidental release of a rocket on the ground, killing a civilian in the village of Salak South, a complete embargo was placed on the carriage of bombs and rockets in these aircraft. The gap was filled by the detachment of two Beaufighters of No 84 Squadron from Tengah to Kuala Lumpur. With its powerful armament of four 20 mm cannon, six .303 machine-guns, eight RPs or two 250 or 500 lb. bombs, each Beaufighter was the offensive equivalent of two Spitfires.

Their first attack, carried out on 12 August 1948, was on a CT camp north of Batu Melintang on the border between Kelantan and Thailand, and was one of a series of strikes designed to intimidate a force of 600 terrorists who were reported to be massing just over the border in readiness to infiltrate. The Beaufighters' first attack reportedly killed thirty terrorists, but this was unconfirmed. On 12 August three more Beaufighters arrived, having been detached from No 45 Squadron at Negombo in Ceylon, and in the following week four strikes were mounted, the heaviest on 17 August when five Beaufighters and five Spitfires (the latter using their cannon only) attacked a CT camp near Bentong in Pahang. Unfortunately this, the biggest strike so far undertaken, resulted in the death of only one terrorist.

At the end of the week's operations No 84 Squadron's two aircraft returned to Tengah in readiness for a move to the Middle East. The three Beaufighters of No 45 Squadron continued operations, and on the night of 22/23 August they carried out the first night strike of the campaign on a target near Parit in Perak. This proved the feasibility of night attacks under moon conditions with the aid of flares, but no further sorties of this nature were flown until July 1950.

The number of offensive air strikes requested by the Security Forces declined in the closing months of 1948, mainly because there was little contact with terrorist forces. The reason for this was that the CT were splitting into smaller groups and withdrawing to secure areas in the jungle, having failed in their bid to establish supremacy in southern Kelantan. The Spitfires of No 60 Squadron returned to Sembawang for a few weeks, but moved up to Kuala Lumpur again after drastic Government measures, including plans for resettlement and deportation, led to an increased flow of information about terrorist locations and a corresponding increase in air-strike activity. Twenty strikes were carried out in December 1948, bringing the total since the start of the campaign to eighty-four.

Up to this point, air strikes had usually been called in after ground forces were in position to ambush terrorists fleeing from the target area. Early in 1949 there was a change in tactics whereby troop movements preceding an attack were disguised, so that the associated air strikes might achieve the maximum element of surprise. On 28 February 1949, using these modified tactics, four Beaufighters and eight Spitfires (the latter now cleared to carry 20 lb fragmentation bombs) carried out a very successful attack on a target near Mengkuang in south Pahang, killing at least fifteen terrorists. Another very successful series of six strikes was flown over a twelve-day period in April 1949, the target lying in the Kuala Langat Forest Reserve area of southern Selangor. Forty-five terrorists were eliminated in these attacks.

The value of offensive air operations in Malaya was now proven without question, and the remainder of 1949 saw a steady increase in offensive air power. On 16 May 1949 the remainder of No 45 Squadron arrived at Kuala Lumpur, and although the Spitfires of No 28 Squadron moved from Sembawang to a new location at Hong Kong that month, their loss was offset by the arrival of No 33 Squadron, with Hawker Tempest F.2 aircraft, at Seletar on 8 August. A week later, the strength of No 60 Squadron was increased from eight to seventeen Spitfires. On 3 September 1949, No 205 Squadron, with Sunderlands, was moved from Ceylon to Seletar, bringing the total air-strike force to seventeen Spitfires, sixteen Tempests, eight Beaufighters and ten Sunderlands. On 6 December, No 45 Squadron exchanged its elderly Beaufighters for Bristol Brigand light bombers, aircraft that were to be dogged by technical troubles throughout their service in Malaya.

In the closing months of 1949, information from surrendered terrorists led to an increase in the number of CT targets available for selection, and for a time the demands made upon the air-strike force outstripped its capability. The biggest strike so far, against a target near Gemas in Negri Sembilan, was carried out on 21 October and involved 62 sorties by Spitfires, Beaufighters, Tempests and Sunderlands of the RAF and by Fireflies and Seafires of Nos 827 and 800 Squadrons of the Fleet Air Arm, which had arrived in the theatre on the aircraft carrier HMS *Triumph*. During the last two months of 1949, 62 strikes, involving 388 sorties, were flown against targets in western and central Malaya. Joint strikes by the RAF and RN continued into the early weeks of 1950, 41 sorties being flown against targets in Negri Sembilan on 1 and 2 January. In all, 58 strikes involving over 300 sorties were carried out during the month.

Many of the strikes were mounted at the request of the police, but on 7 February five civilians were wounded when an air strike was mounted too close to a squatter settlement near Kulai in Johore, and orders were issued by the Federal Police curtailing further police requests of this nature. The restrictions were lifted at a later date, but in the meantime the Communist propaganda machine made much capital out of the unfortunate incident.

On 20 March 1950, eight Avro Lincoln bombers of No 57 Squadron arrived at Tengah on a three-month temporary detachment from their home base of RAF Waddington, near Lincoln. They were followed, on 9 April, by eight Brigands of No 84 Squadron, which were also based at Tengah on indefinite detachment from MEAF. The Lincolns went into action for the first time on 26 March against a jungle target in Negri Sembilan.

The four-engined Lincoln was well-suited to the medium-bomber role in Malaya. Its serviceability record was good, unlike that of most of the other types used in the air campaign; with full tanks it had an endurance of eleven hours at 180 knots; and five aircraft, flying in a close 'vic' formation, could deliver seventy 1,000 lb. bombs in high concentration on designated targets anywhere in the Federation of Malaya by day or by night.

The medium-bomber force in Malaya received a further boost in June 1950, with the arrival of six Lincolns of No 1 Squadron RAAF at Tengah. This unit had been despatched to the theatre as a result of representations made by the UK Government to the Australian Government, that the campaign in Malaya was not merely a matter of internal security of a British colony but an active front in the Cold War against Communism. No 1 Squadron was to remain the backbone of medium-bomber operations in Malaya for the next eight years. The RAF's Lincoln force operated on a rotational basis, with Bomber Command detachments following one another. On 10 July 1950, No 57 Squadron was replaced by eight Lincolns of No 100 Squadron, and these in turn were replaced by eight aircraft of No 61 Squadron on 1 December.

Between 15 March and the beginning of May 1950, the combined air–ground operation known as JACKPOT was launched against No 2 Regiment Malayan Races' Liberation Army (MRLA), which had about 260 terrorists in the field in south-eastern Selangor and northern Negri Sembilan and which was commanded by the notorious terrorist leader Liew Kon Kim. The heaviest air strikes of JACKPOT took place on 14, 15 and 16 April, when offensive support aircraft flew 98 sorties with a Dakota acting as an airborne tactical headquarters. The operations resulted in the elimination of 44 terrorists.

Night bombing operations were resumed on the night of 23/24 July 1950, after an interval of nearly two years, when six Lincolns attacked a jungle area near the Sungkai–Tapah road in Perak, two searchlights being used to provide a datum point for the release of the bombs. On their return to base the bombers dropped reconnaissance flares on selected targets, a practice that became fairly routine as it discouraged terrorists from attacking estates and mines and from ambushing railways.

The use of Lincoln medium bombers of RAF Bomber Command in the Malayan campaign had been the subject of some controversy. The

AOC Malaya, Air Vice-Marshal F. J. Mellersh, was a strong advocate of a greater striking force, and believed that a heavy initial blow could best be achieved by the use of medium bombers, hitting the terrorists hard before they could disperse into the jungle, and a request was made for a force of at least twelve or sixteen Lincolns to be deployed to FEAF. On the other hand, the former AOC Air Command Far East (which had become Far East Air Force in June 1949), Air Marshal Sir Hugh P. Lloyd, who was now AOC-in-Chief Bomber Command, considered that existing strike aircraft were adequate for the task. Moreover, the Lincoln was still the mainstay of Bomber Command's medium-bomber force (the Canberra jet bomber had yet to enter service) and the despatch of the equivalent of two squadrons of these aircraft to the Far East would have had an adverse effect on the Command's training programme. In the end, the Air Ministry agreed that eight Lincolns would be detached to Malaya for a period of two months (later extended to four and then to six months), the aircraft being drawn in rotation from the eighteen Lincoln-equipped squadrons of Bomber Command. The code-name Operation MUSGRAVE was given to these temporary periods of duty, and at the request of the Colonial and Foreign Offices an attempt was made to play down the use of medium bombers in Malaya, because the idea of heavy saturation bombing had an unfortunate link with the Second World War and it was certain that the Communist propaganda machine would exploit it. Moreover, it was by no means certain, when the first Lincolns arrived, that the saturation bombing of jungle areas would be a success. As it turned out, it was.

In mid-1950 the air-strike force had a strength of sixteen Spitfires, sixteen Tempests, sixteen Brigands, fourteen Lincolns and ten Sunderlands. Following the outbreak of the Korean War in June, however, the Sunderlands of No 209 Squadron departed for Iwakuni, in Japan. This was not a serious loss, but at the end of March 1951 the Lincolns of No 61 Squadron left for the United Kingdom at the end of their tour and were not replaced, which had far more serious consequences. This was due to renewed pressure on the Air Ministry by Bomber Command, whose medium-bomber force was reduced to six squadrons of Lincolns, making it hard to maintain the all-important NATO commitment while the Command converted to Canberras and to Boeing B-29 Washingtons, eighty-seven of which were being loaned by the United States as a stop-gap measure.

The loss of the Bomber Command Lincoln detachment was partly offset by increasing the establishment of No 1 Squadron RAAF to eight aircraft and that of Nos 45 and 84 Squadrons to ten Brigands each. However, as two of the fighter squadrons on the order of battle in Malaya were undergoing re-equipment at this time, there was an inevitable reduction in the number of air-strike sorties flown in the first half of 1951. The fourteen Spitfires FR.18s of No 60 Squadron – the last in service with the RAF – were withdraw in December 1950 and January 1951, having carried out 1,800 operational sorties against the terrorists. The squadron re-equipped with de Havilland Vampire FB.5 jet fighter-bombers, and was out of the line until the end of April 1951 for training in its primary role of air defence. The other squadron affected was No 33, whose Tempest Mk 2s had been well-suited to their task, providing a stable firing platform for a reasonable weight of rocket and cannon fire. Moreover, with a range of up to 500 miles they were able to loiter at low level for some time until they were in a position to attack small pinpoint targets with the minimum of compromise in relatively poor weather conditions.

No 33 Squadron carried out many anti-terrorist sorties in the closing months of 1949, but by 1950 the Tempests had become a wasting asset because of low serviceability, and so it was decided to replace them with the de Havilland Hornet F.3. A development of the famous Mosquito, the Hornet was the fastest twin-piston-engined aircraft in the world and had entered RAF service just too late to see service in the Second World War. It carried an armament of four 20 mm cannon, plus eight 60 lb. rockets or two 1,000 lb. bombs. Conversion to the new type was undertaken gradually, so that while No 33 Squadron did not cease operations with its Tempests until June 1951, one flight had already begun flying Hornets in April. By August 1951 the whole squadron was operational with Hornets at Butterworth, although only at three-quarters strength.

The offensive support force was beset by technical troubles throughout 1951. First of all, a Brigand suffered structural failure and crashed, leading to the grounding of the whole Brigand force while investigations into the cause were carried out. It was found that the firing of the aircraft's four 20 mm cannon caused unacceptable airframe stresses, and the use of guns on Brigands was prohibited thereafter, reducing the aircraft's strike potential. Soon afterwards, Vampires experienced problems with their ammunition chute doors, and the guns of the Hornets were restricted when it was found that ejected ammunition links were damaging the tailplane. Finally, the bomb carriers of both Vampires and Hornets developed faults that required design modifications.

Despite the problems, the tempo of air strikes – assisted, when the opportunity arose, by RN aircraft from carriers en route to, or homeward bound from, Korean waters – was maintained at a high level, and operations were attended by some notable successes. At the end of March 1951, strikes in the hilly jungle terrain between Karak and Temerloh in Pahang in support of Operation SABAI drove out a terrorist unit, which was then ambushed by Gurkhas and six CTs killed. This was followed, on 16 June, by Operation WARBLER, which was mounted as part of the Briggs Plan to clear Malaya of terrorists from the south northwards. The operation look place in Johore, and the air forces were used to harass the terrorists by denying them river crossings, escape routes and assembly areas and by attacking clearings and camps which could not immediately be reached by the ground forces. In two months the offensive support force flew 145 air strikes involving 610 sorties, 242 of them in the first week; further strikes, many of them at night, were subsequently mounted against terrorists fleeing from the area of the original operation.

On 14 August 1951, a successful strike by Hornets, Brigands and Vampires on a CT camp near Sitiawan in south-west Perak dislodged a strong force of No 8 Regiment MRLA. Another inaccessible CT camp, in swampland in Kuala Selangor, was attacked by three Brigands on 12 September, and on 8 November this camp was almost obliterated in a further attack by fourteen Brigands, eight Hornets, four Lincolns and a Sunderland. Prior to that, on 6 October 1951, the air forces had been called in to support Operation PURSUIT, which was mounted to catch the terrorists responsible for the ambush and murder of Sir Henry Gurney, the High Commissioner for the Federation of Malaya, on the Kuala Kubu-Gap road. Lincolns and Sunderlands were used to mount an air blockade along a line 5,000 yards long to the east of the scene of the ambush to try and cut off the terrorists' retreat and drive them into contact with ground patrols, but only seven CTs were killed during the operation, which lasted until 21 November.

During 1952, the offensive support force flew more than 4,000 sorties, expending more than 4,000 tons of bombs, 10,000 rockets and 2 million rounds of ammunition in attacks on some 700 targets. One of the biggest efforts was mounted in mid-February during Operation PUMA, when the air-strike force attacked a target area in western Pahang. This area, consisting of thick primary jungle in mountainous terrain, was estimated to be sheltering some 400 terrorists, surrounded by a screen of 300 aboriginal Sakai tribesmen that ruled out any chance of a surprise attack. Between 13 and 15 February, eighteen Lincoln sorties were flown, followed by thirty-five Brigand sorties in the next three days. It was the first time that no ground forces had been involved in such an operation, but because of the nature of the terrain it proved impossible to assess results beyond the fact that considerable damage was caused in the target area.

On 31 January 1952, No 45 Squadron was withdrawn from operations to be converted from Brigands to Hornets, returning in June at half strength, while No 60 Squadron exchanged its Vampire 5s for the later Vampire FB.9 on 24 March. At the end of December, following more structural failures, the Brigands of No 84 Squadron were grounded.

The squadron disbanded on 1 February 1953 but was reformed the same day in MEAF, transferring its numberplate to No 204 Squadron and operating Valetta transport aircraft.

In 1953 the tempo of air-strike operations was greatly reduced. This was the result of a policy change, the main offensive air-support effort now being directed against a small number of pinpoint targets instead of bombing large areas of jungle. In July 1953, however, this policy was revised when a decline in terrorist surrenders showed that area bombing had been an effective weapon after all. With full-scale combined operations being planned with a view to bringing an end to the campaign, additional medium-bomber reinforcements were requested to supplement the effort of No 1 Squadron RAAF. The Air Ministry agreed, and on 1 September the Lincolns of No 83 Squadron arrived at Tengah from RAF Hemswell. Between then and March 1955, detachments of eight Lincolns from Nos 83, 7 and 148 Squadrons were deployed at Tengah for tours of three to five months.

In November 1953, one heavy air strike by the Lincolns of No 1 Squadron RAAF came close to eliminating Chin Peng, the Secretary-General of the Malayan Communist Party. He escaped, but three members of his bodyguard were killed and three wounded. The value of the renewed area-bombing offensive was soon demonstrated when, after one heavy strike by Lincolns, 145 Sakai aborigines appealed for Government protection, providing the Security Forces with valuable information and depriving the terrorists of supply and intelligence support.

The biggest combined operation during this period was Operation SWORD, which was mounted in an area of 100 square miles in the Bongsu Forest Reserve of Southern Kedah between July 1953 and March 1954. In the first week of the operation 37 Lincoln, 237 Hornet and 7 Sunderland sorties were flown. No 33 Squadron had an advantage in that its base at Butterworth was only 30 miles from the target area, and consequently it was able to maintain its Hornets over the target constantly during the hours of daylight. The display of concentrated air power had an excellent effect on the morale of the ground forces, who maintained the offensive after dark with mortar and artillery fire. By the end of Operation SWORD, 36 terrorists had been killed, 19 had been captured or had surrendered, and 106 of their camps had been destroyed.

On 1 January 1955, Nos 205 and 209 Squadrons, which had eight remaining Sunderlands, were amalgamated at Seletar, and on 31 March, Nos 33 and 45 Squadrons, with a total strength of twenty Hornets, were also amalgamated. The combined unit began retraining with sixteen Vampire FB.9s soon afterwards, and in October, renumbered No 45 Squadron, it re-equipped with the more powerful Venom FB.1 and was established at Butterworth with sixteen of these aircraft. At the same time No 33 Squadron, which had served so well in Malaya, reformed at RAF Driffield as a night-fighter unit in RAF Fighter Command. In April 1955, No 60 Squadron also exchanged its Vampires for Venom FB.1s, and in that month the Venoms of No 14 Squadron RNZAF were deployed at Tengah from Cyprus, so that by the end of the year the fighter-bomber squadrons of the offensive support force were equipped entirely with Venoms. This caused a considerable reduction in the number of strike sorties flown in 1955, because the three Venom squadrons had to train in their primary role of air defence.

In February 1955, Canberra jet bombers appeared in FEAF for the first time when a detachment of four aircraft (Mk 6s) from No 101 Squadron, RAF Binbrook, was deployed at Changi under the squadron commander, Squadron Leader W. D. Robertson. After a period of tropical trials, the Canberras moved up-country to Butterworth in order to be closer to their designated targets. On 4 April, the four jet bombers joined eleven Lincolns and twelve Hornets in a strike on an area of jungle on the borders of Negri Sembilan and Selangor, where 200 terrorists were reported to be hiding, but subsequent operations by ground forces found no trace of the enemy.

Although the Canberra had a much higher indicated air-speed (1AS) than the Lincoln, it was found that the same techniques for attacks on area and pinpoint targets could be used without too much modification. Pinpoint targets were all attacked by aircraft flying in 'vic' formation. Having received the target position as a six-figure map reference and the time on target, all further operational planning was done at squadron level, in conjunction with the ground liaison officer, who provided the Army background, explained the need for the strike, told the crews where the enemy had last been seen, and precisely where friendly ground forces were positioned. The target position was first plotted in terms of latitude and longitude on a one-inch map of the area, then replotted on 1:1,000,000 topographical map. The next step was to draw a circle, using the target as a centrepoint, the radius being the distance flown in ten minutes at IAS of 200 knots (in the case of the Canberra) at 4,000 feet above the target height. The direction of attack which was eventually decided upon depended on a careful study of the map features within the circle, also taking into account such factors as the position of the sun at the planned time of the attack, the position of the target in relation to high ground, and the location of friendly ground forces. The required track to be flown was plotted from a point on the edge of the ten-minute circle to the target and a number of easily-recognizable checkpoints were marked on it for the run-in.

The technique called for an Auster marker aircraft to be airborne at H hour minus ten, at a point four minutes' flying time from the target, while the Canberra force was at a position where the track to the target intersected the ten-minute circle. The strike leader would contact the Auster on R/T and call three times, 'Bombing in ten', which was acknowledged. Further calls were made to the Auster at intervals, and as checkpoints came up slight adjustments were made to the timing. At two minutes, by which time the Auster was heading in towards the target, the strike leader called 'Bombing in ninety seconds'. The Auster pilot then dropped his marker flare on the target and broke away at right angles to the attack. As soon as the flare was visible the bomb aimer in the lead aircraft took over and made a normal bombing run.

For an attack on an area target, it first of all had to be decided what bomb pattern was required, so that the stick lengths and the number of runs needed to give the pattern could be calculated. As the areas were invariably jungle-covered country with no distinguishing features the only way to carry out this type of attack was to make timed runs from a point some distance away from the target which could easily be identified from the air. Experience proved the ideal distance to be about 8,000 yards. A suitable datum point, such as a bend in a road or river, or the corner of a rubber plantation, was selected on the one-inch map and then checked against a photographic mosaic. This check was of great importance because the maps tended to be inaccurate, mainly because of the continual expansion of rubber plantations. Also, roads running through the jungle were not always visible from the air.

Having agreed on the datum point, the distance was measured accurately in yards from the datum to the position of the first bomb strike on each run and then the required tracks were decided. This information was given to all crews at briefing, together with the required bomb spacing and speeds; the remaining calculations were completed in the air, after finding a wind within a reasonable distance of the target. Having obtained the wind details from the wind-finding attachment, the heading to make good the required track from datum point to target was calculated together with the ground speed. Ground speeds were then converted into yards per second, and the time in seconds to cover the distance from the datum point to the position of the first bomb strike was calculated. From this figure the time of the bomb fall was subtracted, leaving the 'carry time'. On crossing over the datum point, the stop-watch was started and the bombs released after the required number of seconds had elapsed.

During its four-and-a-half-month detachment in Malaya, No 101 Squadron flew 98 sorties, of which 43 were attacks on pinpoints and 55 on area targets. Cameras were carried on all strikes and a 60 per cent line overlap taken from bomb release to bomb strike. Results analysed by the Joint Air Photographic Interpretation Centres showed a high standard of accuracy, the pinpoint targets in particular being invariably straddled with bomb bursts. This was particularly encouraging, as pinpoint targets were by no means easy to attack successfully. About two minutes before the air strike, the terrorists were warned by the presence of the Auster – although it is interesting to note that the noise of the Canberras could not be heard in this type of terrain more than one minute's flying time away, and in some instances, depending on the wind direction, the bombers were not heard at all.

The times when bombing operations could be carried out were also restricted by the weather factor. At dawn, for example, large areas of stratus covered the country, and in the late afternoon attacks in the mountains might have to be called off because of a large build-up of cumulonimbus cloud. Another handicap was that the majority of terrorist camps tended to be deserted during the daytime; the best time to hit them was at night when they were occupied, but night-bombing operations were restricted to the moon period because the Auster pilot had to map-read his way and use his own local knowledge of the country to find the target. Later, the armaments staff of FEAF developed a time-delay marker, the idea being for the Auster pilot to drop the marker during the day when the terrorists were absent on operations. The strike force would then rendezvous during the darkness and, at the pre-arranged time when the marker was due to ignite, begin the bombing run.

In March 1955 the Bomber Command Lincoln detachments to Malaya ceased, the commitment now being taken over by detachments of six or eight Canberras from Nos 101, 617, 12 and 9 Squadrons. This left No 1 Squadron RAAF as the only unit still operating Lincolns in the theatre.

On 9 September 1955, following an amnesty declaration, all offensive air operations were suspended until late November, when the terrorists, having taken advantage of the respite to build up their forces, launched an attack on Kea Farm New Village in the Cameron Highlands area of northern Pahang. On 25 November Canberras of No 12 Squadron attacked CT camps in the Taiping area of Perak, and three days later Lincolns and Canberras began a ten-day offensive air-support operation in conjunction with five battalions of troops operating in Negri Sembilan, where Yang Kwo, the Vice Secretary-General of the MCP, and Ah Hoi, State Committee Secretary of the Johore Secretariat, were reported to be encamped. During the ten-day period (Operation SATURATION) 752 1,000 lb. bombs were dropped, but with no significant results.

It was a different story on 21 February 1956, when seven Lincolns of No 1 Squadron RAAF and four Canberras of No 12 Squadron carried out Operation KINGLY PILE, an air strike on a CT camp near Kluang in central Johore. The target was successfully straddled by 1,000 lb. bombs and at least twenty-two terrorists were killed, although only fourteen bodies could be identified; eight others had been completely blown to pieces by the explosions. One of the dead terrorists was Goh Peng Tuan, commander of the 7th Independent Platoon MRLA, which was a considerable coup for the Security Forces.

Apart from this, most air strikes in 1956 were flown in support of combined operations which had been in progress for many months, some since the end of 1954. The total number of air strikes mounted in 1956 was 129, less than half the previous year's total. As the strength of the terrorists declined and they turned to the defensive, avoiding contact with the Security Forces, reliable intelligence on their movements became increasingly scarce, and there was a corresponding reduction in offensive air-support activity. It was only rarely that reliable target information became available; in fact, only one accurate pinpoint target became available in the whole of 1957, but the result was one of the most successful air strikes of the campaign.

During 1956, some 545,000 lb. of bombs had been dropped on a supposed encampment of the 3rd Independent Platoon MRLA seven miles north-west of Klawang in Negri Sembilan, but a lack of accurate pinpoints had nullified the effect. The camp was again attacked at the beginning of May 1957 by five Lincolns of No 1 Squadron RAAF and twelve Venoms of No 60 (RAF) and No 14 (RNZAF) Squadrons, which dropped a total of 94,000 lb. of bombs, but because of inaccurate target information this weight of explosive was 250 yards off target. Then, on 15 May, further information was received about the whereabouts of the 3rd Independent Platoon, and 70,000 lb. of bombs were dropped by five Lincolns of No 1 Squadron RAAF in a night strike in the Jelebu district of Negri Sembilan. The attack was entirely successful; four terrorists were killed, including the commander of the 3rd Independent Platoon MRLA, Teng Fook Loong, and his wife. The remaining members of the platoon surrendered to ground forces later in the year after a lengthy seek-and-destroy operation, supported by harassing air strikes.

In November 1957, No 45 Squadron began converting to Canberras, the conversion being undertaken at RAF Coningsby in the UK and the aircraft being ferried to Tengah. In the following year No 14 Squadron RNZAF was replaced by No 75 Squadron RNZAF, which had also re-equipped with Canberra B.2s, and a third Canberra unit, No 2 Squadron RAAF, was deployed at Butterworth in July 1958. The primary role of this squadron was to be available for operations as part of the British Commonwealth Strategic Reserve in South-East Asia, with the secondary role of carrying out attacks in support of ground operations against the terrorists who were still at large in the Malayan jungle, although by this time in greatly depleted numbers. Because of NATO operational commitments and other urgent operational requirements such as the impending Suez crisis, Bomber

Command Canberra detachments to Malaya had ceased in August 1956.

No 2 Squadron RAAF was to remain at Butterworth until early 1967, when it was redeployed to Phan Rang in South Vietnam. Also at Butterworth, from November 1958, was No 3 Squadron RAAF, with F-86 Sabres; this was joined by another Sabre-equipped unit, No 77 Squadron RAAF, in February 1959.

Meanwhile, on 1 September 1958, the medium-bomber commitment in Malaya had ceased with the departure of No 1 Squadron RAAF, which went to RAAF Amberley to re-equip with Canberra B.20s. In its eight-year Malayan tour, No 1 Squadron had dropped 17,500 tons of bombs in more than 3,000 sorties, over half the tonnage of bombs dropped in the entire campaign. It had been credited with killing only sixteen terrorists and destroying between twenty and thirty of their camps, but the psychological impact of its bombing effort on the enemy had far outstripped any material damage it had achieved.

No air strikes at all took place in the first seven months of 1959, but on 13 August several terrorist camps, located by Auster spotter aircraft east of Bentong in northern Pahang, were bombed by Canberras of Nos 2 (RAAF), 45 (RAF) and 75 (RNZAF) Squadrons, while Sabres of Nos 3 and 77 Squadrons RAAF strafed pinpoints that had been marked by an Auster. Four days later, on 17 August 1959, a target on the northern slopes of Bukit Tapah in Perak was attacked by Canberras, marking the last use of offensive air support in the Malayan campaign.

It is almost impossible to assess the results of offensive air support in Malaya in terms of terrorists destroyed. During the first year and a half of the campaign, credible intelligence reports credited strike aircraft with the deaths of 98 terrorists and the wounding of 22 more; a year later this total had risen to 126 terrorists killed and a further 141 confirmed, out of a total of 1,641 CTs eliminated by the Security Forces by the end of 1950. However, these figures do not take into account terrorists who may subsequently have died of wounds inflicted during air attacks.

Unquestionably, the most important effect of the offensive air-support campaign was on morale. Continual harassment from the air had a fearfully demoralizing effect on terrorists who were already suffering from the rigours of life in the jungle, and was the agent that persuaded many to surrender. Air strikes also had a decisive effect on the morale of the civilian population, providing a demonstration of power that persuaded many civilians to resist the terrorists and co-operate with the Security Forces. Finally, and by no means least important, the presence of strike aircraft provided a great uplift to the morale of the troops on the ground, fighting an elusive and ruthless foe in an alien environment.

AIR RECONNAISSANCE

The success of the offensive air-support campaign in Malaya would have been impossible to achieve without efficient and fast-reacting photographic and visual reconnaissance. Throughout the Emergency, almost the whole of the photographic reconnaissance (PR) commitment was fulfilled by No 81 Squadron, which in June 1948 was at Tengah with nine de Havilland Mosquito PR.34s and two Spitfire FR.18s. When the Emergency began, the two Spitfires were based forward at Kuala Lumpur and in June 1949 they were joined by a third which had been converted to the PR role. In March 1950 these three aircraft were transferred to No 60 Squadron as a separate flight, and at the same time the Mosquitos of No 81 Squadron were moved from Tengah to Seletar. Two Spitfire PR.19s were acquired later in the year, and in November 1950 the three Spitfires were transferred back from No 60 Squadron, giving No 81 Squadron a total strength of nine Mosquitos and five Spitfires.

By this time the Spitfires were showing signs of wear, but no replacements could be found for them until December 1953, when five Gloster Meteor PR.10 jets joined No 81 Squadron. The Mosquitos were now down to six in number and continued to serve until 1955, when they were withdrawn. This temporarily reduced the squadron's aircraft strength to six, including one Meteor T.7 trainer, but in 1956 another Meteor PR.10 arrived, together with four Hunting Pembroke C(PR)Mk 1 aircraft, the latter communications aircraft converted for PR work. The Pembrokes were withdrawn in 1958, and at the beginning of 1959, No 81 Squadron, now back at Tengah, was reduced in strength to three PR Meteors and the Meteor T.7.

In October 1959, badly-needed reinforcements arrived in the shape of three Canberra PR.7s and one Canberra T.4 trainer. These aircraft continued to provide the RAF's PR commitment in the peninsula during and after the Emergency.

From May 1955 to October 1956, PR assistance was also provided by Canberra detachments of Nos 542, 540, 82 and 58 Squadrons, No 3 Group, RAF Bomber Command.

The first operational sortie carried out by No 81 Squadron in Malaya in fact took place before the Emergency was declared. On 21 April 1948, a PR Spitfire took off from Taiping in support of a police operation (Operation HAYSTACK) in the Sungei Perak valley, but the sortie was aborted because of bad weather. Regular tactical PR operations began in July 1948, with the detachment of two Spitfires at Kuala Lumpur. There was no real co-ordination or systematic planning at this stage; in fact, for the first two or three months of the campaign all tactical

PR requirements were flown by one Spitfire and one pilot of No 81 Squadron, who once flew for 56 days in succession and carried out 60 sorties, of which 40 were successful. During the first 18 months of the campaign the Spitfires flew a monthly average of 20 to 30 sorties; these were sufficient to meet the demands of the Security Forces, leaving the PR Mosquitos free to continue their task of surveying the 51,000 square miles of Malayan territory so that new and revised maps could be completed as quickly as possible. (The survey programme had been initiated in 1945 on behalf of the Colonial Office, and was accelerated when the Emergency was declared.)

In 1953 the PR aircraft of No 81 Squadron were flying an average of 100 sorties a month, although only about a third of these produced satisfactory results. The Mosquitos were withdrawn from use in 1955, the last operational sortie by this type of aircraft being flown on 21 December. By this time, the use of elaborate camouflage techniques by the terrorists had reduced the amount of intelligence that could be gained from tactical photographic reconnaissance, and from now on most of No 81 Squadron's effort was devoted to obtaining the necessary topographical coverage for ground operations and for carrying out post-strike photography of target areas. The Meteor PR.10s flew about 50 sorties each month from 1956 to the beginning of 1959 to meet this commitment.

The most successful method of detecting terrorist hideouts was visual reconnaissance. In the early weeks of the campaign this was undertaken by Dakota aircraft of Nos 48, 52 and 110 Squadrons and by Spitfires of Nos 28 and 60 Squadrons, while a Sunderland of No 209 Squadron carried out coastal reconnaissance up to a distance of 40 miles from the east coast of Malaya, but by the end of 1948 most of the visual reconnaissance task had been taken over by the Austers of No 656 Squadron as its component flights became operational. The squadron's work during this period consisted of assisting ground patrols in the contact reconnaissance role and of plotting terrorist camps; the Austers also acted as spotters for a naval bombardment and on one occasion in September 1948 the crew of an aircraft of No 1902 Flight, flying in support of the 1st Battalion 6th Gurkha Rifles in the Rambat area of Perak, opened fire with a Bren gun against a band of fleeing terrorists.

No 656 Squadron's visual reconnaissance commitments increased steadily during 1949 and 1950, although communications work occupied much of its time. The gap between the two tasks narrowed in 1951, and in the following year visual reconnaissance (VR) occupied half the squadron's total task. The normal VR method employed was to scan the jungle with the aid of binoculars from a height of 3,000 feet, the aircraft flying in a straight line so that any terrorists in the vicinity would assume that it was on a communications sortie. By 1953 the terrorists had become very nervous of air reconnaissance, and were likely to make a rapid move out of the area if they suspected that they were under surveillance. The terrorists were now beginning to withdraw into the deep jungle of Malaya's spinal ridge, and much of No 656 Squadron's effort was devoted to locating the cultivation plots on which the enemy depended for survival. In order to spot these small patches, the Austers had to descend to about 1,000 feet over the jungle, and from 1954 the MCP directed that the aircraft were to be engaged with small arms and light automatic fire whenever possible. This diversion from the MCP's usual policy of evasion was, in itself, a clear indication of the threat posed to the CTs by the spotter aircraft, but there was only one recorded instance of an aircraft actually coming under fire, and no damage was sustained.

By the end of 1954, No 656 Squadron, with 31 Austers on strength, was devoting two-thirds of its sorties to the visual reconnaissance task. In the following year, however, the sortie rate began to decline for want of targets, the terrorists having now partly abandoned their policy of growing food in jungle plots. Nevertheless, between March and August 1955 the Austers located 155 confirmed terrorist camps, 77 possible terrorist camps, 313 cultivations, 31 re-cultivations, 194 clearings that had probably been made by terrorists, and 21 aborigine farms that were under terrorist domination. Also in 1955, the squadron – which recorded its 100,000th flying hour in Malaya at the end of the year – flew 100 observation sorties in support of the guns of the 25th Field Regiment and the 1st Singapore Regiment, Royal Artillery, and those of HMS *Concord*, HMS *Comus* and HMS *Newcastle*, which were supporting ground forces engaged in Operation NASSAU in the Kuala Langat area of Selangor.

In 1958, No 656 Squadron became part of the Army Air Corps, and by the end of that year only two flights of Austers were still occupied on FIREDOG tasks. On the Thai border, No 7 Reconnaissance Flight located a number of terrorist camps which were still occupied, and in July 1958, flying in support of the 22nd Special Air Service Regiment, provided valuable information for Operation BOULDER, which was mounted east of Grik in northern Perak. In southern Perak, No 2 Reconnaissance Flight operated in support of the Police Special Branch which was rounding up terrorists in the area, and later flew from Alor Star in support of the 1st and 2nd Federal Infantry Brigades during 1959.

AIR-STRIKE PLANNING AND PROCEDURES

Throughout the Malayan Emergency, air-strike planning was hampered by a lack of accurate target intelligence. Informers were the main source of target intelligence, but many of them were of low mentality and were unable to read maps or to assess distances correctly. Attempts to follow up informers' reports by sending out Security Forces patrols almost invariably resulted in the terrorists being alerted, in which case they simply moved elsewhere.

Another problem, at least in the early days of the Emergency, was that ground force commanders were not yet aware of the full potential of air-strike action in support of their operations. The situation began to improve when RAF intelligence officers were attached to State Police Headquarters, and also sent out on ground force patrols to encourage better liaison. Until November 1949 air strikes were arranged on an *ad hoc* basis by personal agreement between Army and Air Force commanders, but after this date they were ordered through the combined Land/Air Operations Room at GHQ Malaya District, Kuala Lumpur, which was eventually expanded to become the Joint Operations Centre in 1954.

The overall offensive campaign against the terrorists was planned by the Director of Operations Committee after 1950, and was executed at state and settlement level by the local War Executive Committees. Requests for air support were originated by company or police circle and channelled through battalion or district and then brigade or State Police Headquarters to the Joint Operations Centre (JOC). As the campaign progressed, this somewhat unwieldy procedure was circumvented when necessary by authorizing Air Support Signals Units, working in operational areas, to pass requests direct from ground patrols or reconnaissance aircraft to the airfield concerned, enabling briefing to be carried out and the strike aircraft to be armed while the necessary permission for the strike was obtained from the JOC. From 1955, under certain circumstances – when only air power was available to maintain pressure on the terrorists, for example – the officers commanding RAF Tengah and Butterworth were made responsible for planning and executing air-strike operations in defined areas, and some Army units were permitted, for limited periods to request offensive air support directly from the strike wings without prior permission from the JOC.

Before an air strike could be mounted, a strict target clearance procedure had to be followed. The necessity for stringent safeguards to protect the civilian population and friendly ground forces was underlined by the very few unfortunate incidents that occurred during the campaign. The attack by a Beaufighter close to a settlement in Johore on 7 February 1950, in which five civilians were wounded, has already been mentioned; there was a more serious incident in November that year, when a combination of bad weather and faulty bomb-loading techniques led to a Lincoln dropping its bombs 600 yards short of the edge of the target near Rawang in central Selangor, killing twelve civilians and injuring twenty-six others, and in August 1953 a premature bomb release by a Canberra through an electrical fault killed a British officer and seven other ranks in the Tasek Bera area of Pahang.

Even when attacking remote jungle areas, great care had to be taken to avoid inflicting casualties on the Sakai aborigines, even though some were known to be supporting the terrorists under duress. This meant that native villages in the danger area had to be cleared prior to a strike going in, which in itself often alerted the terrorists and gave them an opportunity to disperse. As a general rule, no civilians or troops were permitted within an area measuring 6,000 yards by 4,000 yards, the target being at the centre, although from 1956, when better target location devices were available, this was reduced to an area of 2,000 yards by 1,000 yards for bombing attacks and 500 yards square for strafing attacks.

An absolute embargo was placed on air strikes against inhabited or cultivated areas, except of course terrorist camps and plots, and any crew unlucky enough to hit a rubber plantation was liable to be court-martialled. Attacks on certain areas of jungle were also prohibited for fear of damage to local sawmills.

In the early stages of the campaign, local control of air strikes was often provided by an Army Contact Car ('Rover Joe'), using the technique that had been developed for use by fighter-bombers of the Second Tactical Air Force in Europe during the latter part of the Second World War. Information from 'Rover Joe' would be transmitted to an orbiting Dakota, which would call up the attacking forces, assess the local weather and mark the target. By 1951, however, most attacks were carried out by aircraft with no direct links with the ground forces, although aircraft remained in constant communication with the Air Control Centre Malaya during a strike.

Apart from marker flares, certain other devices were used at a later stage to designate terrorist camps. In 1957, the Operational Research Staff developed a small radio transmitter, known as Lodestone, which emitted a continuous signal on a pre-set frequency for twenty-four hours. Lodestone was positioned by a ground patrol and its signal could be detected and fixed by an Auster at a range of 5,000 yards, the fix being accurate to within 100 yards. The biggest problem with Lodestone lay in placing it within an optimum distance of 300 yards from a well-guarded terrorist camp, and it was not used frequently.

From 1956, air strikes were carried out with the aid of a Target Director Post, a self-contained mobile radar unit that transmitted a narrow beam over the target. The strike aircraft flew down this beam and received a signal to bomb at a distance from the transmitter that was calculated on the basis of various factors such as air speed, bomb ballistics, height, stick length and slant ranges. The use of this technique meant that sustained attacks could be carried out by day or night in all weathers. The system was similar to the SHORAN blind-bombing navigation system used successfully by US Air Force B-26s and B-29s in the Korean War.

Towards the end of the air campaign, operational research was turning to applied science in the quest for accurate target marking and locating devices. Trials were carried out with infra-red apparatus aimed at detecting the enemy's camp-fires, but this was never used operationally in Malaya.

AIR WEAPONS

The most effective weapon used in the Malayan campaign was the 1,000 lb. HE nose-fused bomb, which was first employed in 1950 following the arrival of Lincoln medium bombers in the theatre. This weapon, which had a mean area of effectiveness of 75,000 square feet, was dropped by Lincolns and Canberras. The 500 lb. HE nose-fused bomb was the next most commonly used weapon; it was employed from August 1948 and had a mean area of effectiveness of 15,000 square feet. Another very viable weapon, with a mean area of effectiveness of 1,000 square feet, was the 20 lb. fragmentation bomb. The noise of its detonation was not much less than that of a 500 lb. weapon, and, since a Sunderland could carry a load of 190, its effect on terrorist morale was considerable. Unfortunately, since only the Sunderland was capable of carrying the 20 lb. in sufficient quantities, it was not used in great numbers, despite its excellent potential as a harassing weapon and the fact that a load of 190, scattered over a terrorist camp, probably had a greater chance of killing CTs than a stick of 1,000 lb. bombs.

The biggest weapon used in the Malayan campaign was the 4,000 lb. HE bomb, but it could not be dropped without the express permission of the High Commissioner for the Federation of Malaya and its blast effect in jungle terrain was not proportionate to its size. It was first used in May 1953, during Operation COMMODORE in Johore, but very few were dropped during the campaign.

Rocket projectiles were widely used. They were certainly more accurate against defined pinpoint targets than bombs, and when followed up by strafing attacks with 20 mm cannon they were much feared by the terrorists, but they had a big disadvantage in that their semi-armour-piercing 60 lb. warheads would usually pass through target buildings and penetrate into the ground before exploding, negating some of their effectiveness.

The Operational Research Section of AHQ Malaya tried out other air weapons during the campaign. One was napalm, which was dropped in 200 lb. canisters and exploded by static line, but its effectiveness in thick jungle was very limited and localized and it was not used operationally. Similarly, trials were also carried out with depth charges as potential blast weapons, but that idea too was abandoned.

Throughout the campaign in Malaya, the most effective combination of aircraft and weapon remained the Avro Lincoln and the 1,000 lb. nose-fused bomb. It was also the most economical, a factor that had to be taken into account when planning air-strike operations, because the cost of air weapons accounted for about one-quarter of the total cost of flying operations in support of FIREDOG.

10

AIR TRANSPORT SUPPORT

Throughout the Malayan campaign, the medium-range transport commitment was fulfilled by four RAF squadrons, Nos 48, 52, 110 and the Far East Communications Squadron, supported from time to time by No 38 Squadron RAAF and No 41 Squadron RNZAF. Initially, all of these squadrons were equipped with Dakota aircraft.

The first supply-dropping operations were carried out in April 1948, before the Emergency was declared, in support of Operation HAYSTACK in northern Perak. A Dakota of No 110 Squadron was positioned at Taiping, as part of the RAF task force, and made its first supply drop on 25 April. This aircraft made regular supply drops to the ground forces every three days until 27 May, when the Taiping task force was withdrawn and a new one established at Kuala Lumpur following the declaration of the Emergency.

Dakotas of No 110 Squadron rotating through Kuala Lumpur made small-scale supply drops to Security Forces at intervals during June and July 1940, but it was not until the terrorists began to withdraw into the jungle after their initial offensive, and trained jungle troops were sent in after them, that the air-supply effort increased. Strangely enough, given the fact that air supply had proved so vital during the campaign in Burma only three years earlier, the Army authorities in Malaya were slow to realize its advantages; the police, on the other hand, readily appreciated that air supply was by far the best method of maintaining remote outposts, and in July and early August two such posts in north Kelantan were supplied almost entirely from the air by No 110 Squadron.

In August 1948, the Dakotas of No 110 Squadron carried out fourteen supply drops to 'Shawforce', engaged in anti-terrorist operations in Pahang and Kelantan, as well as dropping supplies to Security Forces operating elsewhere. During these operations one Dakota crashed during a supply drop to a police post at Batu Melintang, with the loss of all five crew. On 12 November 1948 a second Dakota crashed near Serendah in Selangor, again with the loss of five crew, including the squadron commander. This reduced No 110 Squadron's strength to six aircraft, and on 21 November the unit was replaced at Kuala Lumpur by No 52 Squadron, having dropped some 42,000 lb. of supplies since the outbreak of the Emergency. A further 20,000 lb. of supplies were dropped by No 52 Squadron before the end of the year.

By the beginning of 1949, the rapid expansion of the police forces enabled large-scale anti-terrorist operations to be mounted in the jungle areas. In January, the 2nd Gurkha Rifles mounted Operation GARGOYLE on the borders of Perak, Pahang and Kelantan, and in one week, from the 22nd to the 29th, the Dakotas of No 52 Squadron dropped 35,920 lb. of supplies to this force. In February, the squadron operated in support of Operation HOLIDAY, which was mounted in conjunction with the Thai police on the northern borders of Kedah and Perlis. Operation NAWAB, which was mounted in central Kedah in March, contributed to the increased demand for air supply, and during the first three months of the year 156,000 lb. of supplies were delivered in 80 drops, twice the total delivered during the previous six months.

From April to July 1949, sixty-eight Dakota sorties were flown in support of Operations RAMILLIES, BLENHEIM, SPITFIRE and SARONG, which were mounted against a force of more than 300 terrorists of No 5 Regiment MRLA in north Pahang and Kelantan. In July, the eight Dakotas of No 48 Squadron replaced those of No 52 Squadron at Kuala Lumpur, and these continued to meet the air-supply demand, flying in support of Operations SNOW WHITE and DANIEL in Pahang and Negri Sembilan, PINTAIL and WIDGEON in Perak, PATHFINDER and OVERALL in Kedah, LEMON and PLUNDER in Selangor, and LEO in Johore. In October 1949, No 48 Squadron dropped over 400,000 lb. of supplies during 200 sorties over 206 dropping zones, figures which were not to be surpassed until the campaign reached its peak in 1951.

The pattern of air supply remained the same throughout 1950. No 110 Squadron returned to Kuala Lumpur for a further tour at the beginning of the year and assumed the regular commitment of supply drops to police posts, with larger drops as required in support of operations in the jungle. The most intensive month was April, when the Dakotas flew seventy sorties in support of Operation CARP in the area east of Ipoh, in Perak, and fifty-two sorties in support of Operation JACKPOT in Negri Sembilan and south Selangor against No 2 Regiment MRLA.

Meanwhile, in September 1949, a Dakota flight of No 41 Squadron RNZAF had arrived at Changi, and in December one of the aircraft was deployed at Kuala Lumpur to assist with supply-dropping operations. In June 1950 a flight of No 38 Squadron RAAF also arrived at Changi, its Dakotas positioning forward at Kuala Lumpur for supply-dropping operations as required. Both these flights completed their first tour of duty at Kuala Lumpur on 19 July 1951 and were replaced by No 110

Squadron, now engaged in its third operational tour. In the three months during which they had been at Kuala Lumpur as complete units, as distinct from individual aircraft detachments, the Australians and New Zealanders had dropped 916,632 lb. of supplies.

Early in 1951, two Vickers Valetta twin-engined transports arrived in Malaya for tropical trials. These aircraft were assigned to No 48 Squadron, whose re-equipment with Valettas was completed by 1 April. No 52 Squadron's conversion to the Valetta was also completed in September 1951, and the Dakota elements of the Far East Communications Squadron also converted to the Valetta in November. The conversion was not without its problems, because for some time the Valettas were able to achieve a serviceability rate of only 55 per cent, compared with the elderly Dakota's 75 per cent. Once the technical problems had been resolved, however, the Valetta proved well-suited to the task in hand. It had better forward and downward visibility than the Dakota and also a steeper climbing angle, which made climbing away from dropping zones in narrow valleys a less hazardous undertaking. Fortunately, although the Dakota flight of No 41 Squadron RNZAF was withdrawn from Malaya for re-equipment in November 1950, the four Dakotas of No 38 Squadron RAAF remained and were once again deployed at Kuala Lumpur in November 1951 to compensate for the low availability of the Valettas. No 110 Squadron also began to re-equip with the latter aircraft in October 1951.

In January 1952, the transport support force was heavily engaged in dropping supplies to Security Forces elements which had become isolated because of extensive flooding throughout the Federation, and in the following month the Valettas made operational supply drops for the first time in Malaya in support of Operation HELSBY near the borders of Perak with Thailand. During the remainder of 1952, the RAF Valettas and RAAF Dakotas dropped a monthly average of nearly 250,000 lb. of supplies, about 70 per cent of which were dropped into jungle clearings in support of offensive operations by the Security Forces and the remainder to the thirteen police posts which were being supplied by air on a regular basis.

In the first half of 1953, the volume of supplies dropped rose to a daily average of 12,000 lb. a day in May and June, mainly because of the need to supply – and in some cases drop heavy equipment to – several permanent police forts that were being constructed in deep-jungle areas. In addition, the transport support force was heavily involved in dropping supplies to Security Forces engaged in a large-scale operation, or series of operations, designed to sweep the terrorists from Federation territory. From July 1953 to March 1954 two infantry battalions were almost continuously deployed on Operation SWORD in the Bongsu Forest Reserve of southern Kedah, while four more battalions were engaged in Operation VALIANT from October to December 1953. These operations took place in extremely different terrain, and in many cases air supply was difficult and dangerous, with dropping zones at heights of up to 5,000 feet and surrounded by cloud-covered peaks rising to 7,000 feet. Although several sorties were sometimes required to deliver one load of supplies, the transport forces never failed to meet their commitment. Almost 4.5 million lb. of supplies were dropped during 1953.

In all cases, requests for air supply were radioed from jungle patrols to Army or Police District Headquarters, who passed them on to the Joint Operations Centre at Kuala Lumpur for allocation of tasks, and also to No 55 Air Despatch Company RASC at Kuala Lumpur, who were responsible for packing the supplies, attaching parachutes and providing the necessary air despatchers. In 1954, to meet the increased supply commitment, No 55 Air Despatch Company was re-established with two complete platoons for air supply, and plans were laid for deploying up to fourteen Valettas at Kuala Lumpur to meet the demands of special operations.

In July 1954 the biggest combined operation of the Emergency, Operation TERMITE, was mounted in northern Perak, and in the first two days six Valettas dropped 27,000 lb. of supplies into three dropping zones that had been prepared by personnel of the 22nd Special Air Service Regiment. In all, 58,787 lb. of supplies were delivered by air to the ground forces in the first week of the operations. Further commitments in the second half of the year, mainly in support of Operations HAWK and APOLLO in Pahang and AJAX in Johore, raised the monthly average of supplies dropped to more than 650,000 lb. The total for the year was nearly 6.8 million lb.

With large numbers of troops deployed on protracted operations in the jungle, 1955 was a year of extremely heavy commitment for the transport support force, but the arrival of four Bristol Freighters of No 41 Squadron RNZAF in June 1955 went some way towards relieving the pressure. Operating initially from Changi, these aircraft were to remain part of the Far East Transport Wing until the end of the campaign, and operated from Kuala Lumpur from November 1957. The total weight of supplies dropped in 1955 reached 7.8 million lb. a record for the entire Emergency.

Air-supply operations continued along similar lines during 1956, although with a reduction of some 20 per cent in the supply effort. Many sorties were flown in support of the 22nd Special Air Service Regiment, patrolling in deep jungle with the object of preventing the establishment of terrorist camps.

On 1 May 1957, the Valettas of No 48 Squadron were replaced by eight four-engined Handley Page Hastings transports. One of these aircraft had already been in service with the Far East Communications Squadron since 1953, and now a second was added. Contrary to some predictions, the Hastings proved successful in the tactical supply role in Malaya; the position of the navigator in the nose of the aircraft enabled supply drops into small jungle clearings to be carried out with great accuracy. It carried a maximum payload of 9,000 lb. – twice as much as the Dakota and Valetta – and four packs could be released simultaneously through the aircraft's double doors. Its main disadvantage was that its wide turning circle made it unsuitable for operations over mountainous terrain, which was where most tactical supply drops were carried out during the latter stages of the campaign.

On 31 December 1957, No 110 Squadron, which had served continuously in Malaya for more than ten years, was disbanded, although it would re-form six months later as a transport helicopter unit. By this time, the air-supply commitment in Malaya in direct support of the anti-terrorist campaign was being met by three Valettas of No 52 Squadron and two Bristol Freighters of No 41 Squadron RNZAF, all based at Kuala Lumpur. Most ground operations were now taking place in Perak and Johore, which involved a considerably increased sortie time for the air-transport task force, but the Valettas and Bristol Freighters had sufficient endurance to meet their commitments, which now involved occasional heavy drops of 4.2-inch mortar ammunition. The most intensive month of 1958 was August, when 500,000 lb. of supplies were dropped in support of Operation TIGER in south Johore.

During 1959 the transport support force at Kuala Lumpur continued to operate in support of anti-terrorist actions in northern Malaya. By now the Valettas were beginning to show signs of strain, but some relief was granted when the task of supplying police outposts and jungle forts was taken over by the Royal Malayan Air Force, using Pioneer aircraft. In January and February 1960, the Army, advised of the transport support force's problems with the Valettas, took steps to supply the bulk of its forces in the jungle by other means; this enabled the Valetta force to be brought up to strength once again, and in March and April 1960 some 500,000 lb. of supplies were dropped to units of the 28th Commonwealth Infantry Brigade, operating in Perak (Operation BAMBOO).

In May, the 1st Battalion The Royal Australian Regiment, which had been taking part in BAMBOO, was withdrawn to be redeployed elsewhere, and the air-supply demand fell as a consequence. It rose again to about 200,000 lb. a month in June 1960, when the 3rd East Anglian Regiment was deployed in operations in Perak, and in the following month No 52 Squadron moved from Kuala Lumpur to RAAF Butterworth in order to be closer to this operational area. This was the last official month of the Emergency, but air supply continued at the rate of 200,000 lb. a month as the RAF continued to support Security

Forces in the border area of northern Perak during the remainder of 1960.

In addition to its supply commitment, the medium-range transport force in Malaya also carried out other tasks such as paratrooping, described elsewhere in this book, scheduled passenger services and casualty evacuation. In 1950 and 1951, the Far East Transport Wing made several flights from Changi to Iwakuni in Japan to repatriate troops wounded in Korea. A number of airlifts of troops and police were carried out, mainly between May and September 1948, when most of the available trained forces had been deployed.

Of the many airfields in Malaya, only seventeen were capable of operating medium-range transport aircraft, and a great deal of the sustained effort was supported by short-range types. Of these, the most ubiquitous were the Austers of No 656 Squadron, whose reconnaissance and target-marking tasks have already been described. Austers could use all of the sixty-eight light-aircraft strips which were available in the Federation by the summer of 1955.

The problem with the Auster was that it could carry only one passenger. If a military commander wished to take members of his staff along with him on a visit to an operational area, more than one Auster had to be provided, which imposed an unacceptable strain on No 656 Squadron's resources. There was an obvious requirement for a multi-seat light transport aircraft, and investigations were made into the possibility of purchasing the Canadian de Havilland Beaver, but the necessary dollar funds were not available. In the end the choice fell on the Scottish Aviation Pioneer, which could carry four passengers, 800 lb. of freight or two stretcher cases, and which could operate from nearly all the improvised light-aircraft strips in Malaya. In fact, the short take-off and landing characteristics of the Pioneer were better than those of the Auster. It also had a very low landing speed of 25 knots.

By October 1953, three Pioneers were in service with No 1311 Transport Flight of No 303 Helicopter Wing at Seletar, which became the Support Flight of No 267 Squadron on 15 February 1954. The squadron's Pioneer strength was later built up to eight aircraft, and by the middle of 1955 the Pioneers were regularly carrying over 500 passengers, 30,000 lb. of freight and ten casualties into and out of jungle airstrips every month on an average of 400 forty-minute sorties. The overall task included weekly supply visits to eight jungle forts. In addition to the Pioneers, No 267 Squadron also operated five Percival Pembroke twin-engined communications aircraft, two Austers and three Dakotas, as well as a pair of Harvards for communications work.

On 1 November 1958, No 267 Squadron was renumbered No 209 Squadron. In addition to the aircraft mentioned above (with the exception of the aged Harvards, which had been withdrawn in 1956), its establishment now included five Twin Pioneers. The squadron continued to operate both single- and twin-engined Pioneers on light transport and communications duties from Seletar until it was disbanded in December 1968, by which time most of the light transport work in Malaysia had been taken over by aircraft of the Royal Malayan Air Force.

11

HELICOPTER SUPPORT OPERATIONS

The first helicopter type to be used in the Malayan campaign was the Westland-built S51 Dragonfly, three of which were released from service with the Royal Navy to form the Far East Casualty Air Evacuation Flight at Seletar on 1 April 1950. The flight moved to Changi on 22 May 1950 and by May 1952 was operating five Dragonflies in the casualty evacuation role. However, one of these aircraft was totally destroyed in an accident, and the others were plagued by growing unserviceability problems, so that by the beginning of 1953 the flight was no longer able to perform its task. It was disestablished on 2 February 1953.

Meanwhile, in October 1952, it had been decided to re-form No 194 Squadron, which had carried out light transport and casualty evacuation duties in the Far East during the Second World War, as a short-range helicopter transport squadron. Re-formed at Royal Naval Air Station Sembawang on 2 February 1953, it had an establishment of nine Dragonfly HC2s. Also at Sembawang, having arrived there on 8 January 1953, was No 848 Naval Air Squadron, equipped with ten Sikorsky S-55 medium helicopters which had been supplied by the USA under the Mutual Defence Assistance Programme.

On 2 February 1953, Nos 194 and 848 Squadrons were brought under the control of the newly-formed No 303 (Helicopter) Wing at Sembawang. A detachment of three S-55s and two Dragonflies was deployed to Kuala Lumpur to carry out tactical troop movements and casualty evacuation in north and central Malaya, while three more S-55s and two Dragonflies remained at Sembawang, the other four S-55s being held in reserve. Operational control of the whole helicopter force was vested in Advanced AHQ Malaya, although for practical purposes, during operations, it was assigned to Air Control Teams that were attached to Army formation headquarters. On 1 May 1953, No 303 Wing moved from Sembawang to Kuala Lumpur; on 15 February 1954 it was disbanded and the two constituent helicopter squadrons became part of the RAF Kuala Lumpur Flying Wing.

In April 1954, No 194 Squadron began to receive the Bristol Sycamore HR14 helicopter as a progressive replacement for the Dragonflies, which were now suffering badly from attrition. It was clear by now that the size of the RAF/RN helicopter force in Malaya was insufficient to meet the demands that were being made on it; the Director of Operations report for 1954 estimated that a minimum establishment of fourteen medium and fourteen light helicopters, with four of each in reserve, was required to meet a commitment of airlifting two infantry companies in different areas of the Federation in any one day, and also to airlift the Federal Reserve Battalion of four companies as required, in order to maintain deep-jungle operations in pursuit of the terrorists. In addition, helicopter support involving six airlifts of ninety men each would be required against targets of opportunity, and there was a regular commitment to fly in relief forces to the jungle forts.

By mid-1954, with nearly two years of continuous operations taking their toll on the small helicopter force, the situation was critical. On 28 August, out of a nominal strength of ten S-55s and twelve Dragonflies in Malaya, only one S-55 and one Dragonfly were available for operations. In order to maintain at least some helicopter support, the tour of operations of No 848 Squadron, which was to have ended in August 1954, was extended to April 1955. However, it was not until 18 October 1954 that some real relief arrived in the form of two Sycamores, nine Whirlwind HC4s of No 155 Squadron RAF and five RN Whirlwinds on the aircraft carrier HMS *Glory*, bringing the daily availability to fourteen light helicopters and nine medium helicopters.

The relief was short-lived, mainly because of the poor performance of the Whirlwind. This Westland-built version of the S-55 was a poor, over-heavy copy of the original, and when it first arrived in Malaya it could carry only three troops and would not operate economically above 3,000 feet. It was also difficult to maintain, and during its operational life in Malaya its average serviceability was less than 50 per cent compared with 80 to 90 per cent in the case of the S-55.

Negotiations with the US Government for the provision of fifteen more S-55s proved abortive, so it was decided to retain the S-55s of No 848 Squadron in Malaya for the remainder of their useful lives and to make provision for one extra passenger in the Whirlwinds by removing all unnecessary equipment. No 848 Squadron's S-55s, in fact, continued to service until 10 December 1956, when they were withdrawn following a series of accidents.

At the end of 1955 the helicopter force in Malaya comprised seventeen Whirlwinds and S-55s, with three in reserve, and eleven Sycamores and Dragonflies, also with three in reserve. It was just enough to meet all reasonable demands for helicopter support, but on the whole the position was very unsatisfactory. With the withdrawal of No 848

Squadron at the end of 1956, the entire helicopter commitment in Malaya was met by seventeen Whirlwinds of No 155 Squadron and fourteen Sycamores of No 194 Squadron, the latter unit having relinquished the last of its worn-out Dragonflies in October.

Demands for helicopter support became fewer in 1957, which was fortunate since the Whirlwinds were suffering from a series of technical troubles. This led to a recommendation that the Whirlwinds should be progressively replaced by Sycamores, and the conversion of No 155 Squadron began on 1 December 1957. Conversion was slow and suffered a setback in November 1958, when a defect was found in the main rotor blade of the Sycamore and all these aircraft were grounded for some time, placing a severe strain on the rest of the helicopter force.

A second grounding occurred on 27 April 1959, following a crash, and when Nos 155 and 194 Squadrons were amalgamated on 3 June 1959 to form No 110 Squadron, they had a total of only five Whirlwinds with which to meet their commitments.

The addition of more Whirlwinds brought No 110 Squadron up to an establishment of eight aircraft on 1 September 1959, when it moved to RAAF Butterworth for operations in support of ground forces in the Thailand border area of northern Perak. It was still operating in this area, although to a very limited degree, at the end of the Emergency.

CASUALTY EVACUATION BY HELICOPTER

During the campaign in Malaya, helicopters of the Royal Air Force and Royal Navy evacuated 5,000 casualties, many of whom would certainly have died without prompt assistance, from the Security Forces' operational areas. By no means all were battle casualties; many were attributed to a wide variety of other causes such as snake bites, dysentery, fever, jaundice and appendicitis.

The first casualty to be evacuated by helicopter in Malaya was a wounded policeman who was flown from a police outpost in southern Johore and taken to Johore Hospital by Dragonfly helicopter on 6 June 1950. On 15 June 1950 the first military casualty to be evacuated by helicopter was flown from Segamat airstrip, which had been rendered unusable by fixed-wing aircraft because of heavy rain, to RAF Changi, and on 20 June a Gurkha soldier with severe toothache was evacuated from the jungle near Kluang in Johore. By the end of 1950 helicopters had lifted twenty-six casualties, almost always with commendable speed; on 13 October, for example, four members of a patrol of the 1st Battalion The Worcestershire Regiment, including two stretcher cases, were evacuated to Segamat airstrip from a clearing to the north-east in one hour and forty-five minutes. From Segamat they were taken by road to the British Military Hospital at Kluang, a journey of 35 miles. All survived, and one man, who was suffering from gangrene, certainly owed his life to the speedy evacuation by helicopter.

In 1951, fifty-five casualties were lifted by helicopter, with an average of four or five a month, and on 25 October the Casualty Air Evacuation Flight suffered its first loss when a Dragonfly crashed while attempting to fly out of a small clearing in deep primary jungle. More Dragonflies were added to the Flight in the first half of 1952, enabling more casualties to be evacuated from the jungle. One helicopter was detached to the operational area while the others remained at Changi, one being maintained at permanent standby to answer emergency calls from anywhere in the Federation.

In 1952 the number of casualties lifted by helicopter rose to 168. Of these, 44 were flown out in February and March, mainly as a result of calls for assistance from ground forces engaged in Operation HELSBY in the Belum valley of northern Perak. Three times as many casualties were evacuated by helicopter in 1952 as had been in the previous year; in fact, the number of casualties sustained by the Security Forces was actually declining. Battle casualties averaged four or five a month; the remainder were due to sickness or injury sustained during prolonged jungle operations. On one occasion, helicopters were used to evacuate the seriously injured survivors of a train crash in a remote part of Kelantan.

Casualty evacuation by helicopter really came into its own in 1953, with the advent of No 194 Squadron's Dragonflies and the S-55s of No 848 Squadron. In November the helicopters carried out 85 casualty evacuations in support of Operation VALIANT in the deep jungle of north-west Pahang; most of the casualties were suffering from dysentery, scrub typhus and other jungle diseases. In the course of 1953 the S-55s lifted a total of 280 casualties and the Dragonflies 213.

The number of casualties lifted by helicopter continued to rise steadily, reaching 743 in 1954 and 793 in the following year. In fact 1955 proved to be the peak year of the campaign, but over 600 casualties were flown out of jungle areas in each of the next three years; in 1956, for example, the Sycamores of No 194 Squadron evacuated 500 casualties, including the squadron's 1,500th since its arrival in Malaya.

TROOPLIFTING OPERATIONS BY HELICOPTER

The airlifting of troops by helicopter into operational areas was the most significant development in air-transport support that occurred during the Malayan Emergency. The first major helicopter trooplift of the campaign took place in February 1952, when a single Dragonfly of the Far East Casualty Air Evacuation Flight, piloted by Flight Lieutenant J. R. Dowling, made several sorties to lift seventeen men of the 1st Battalion

The Cameronians, plus one captured terrorist, from a swamp in the Ulu Bernam area of north-west Selangor, when rising water threatened to cut them off. The soldiers were all suffering badly from fatigue and sickness after spending twenty-nine days in swamp country, and it would have taken a fortnight for help to reach them by surface transport.

In the following month, several army commanders, civilian administrators and doctors were flown into and out of the Belum area of northern Pahang during Operation HELSBY, the helicopters also lifting some sick and elderly refugees. These two operations proved the feasibility of using helicopters for lifting numbers of personnel into operational areas, but it was not until the advent of No 848 Squadron and its S-55s at the beginning of 1953 that the idea really became a practical possibility.

No 848 Squadron carried out its first operational trooplift on 16 February 1953 during Operation WELLINGTON II, when three S-55s lifted twelve men of the 1st Battalion The Worcestershire Regiment and a surrendered terrorist into a small peninsula south of Port Swettenham in Selangor in an attempt to capture a local District Committee member of the MCP. Although the operation failed in its objective, it proved that troops could be lifted by helicopter at short notice without previous experience of this type of air-transport support.

Over 300 helicopter trooplifting sorties were flown during the next two months, mostly by No 848 Squadron. The biggest effort came on 24 May, when eight S-55s flying in support of Operation COMMODORE north-east of Kluang in Johore lifted 564 troops over a 9-mile distance into the jungle in an attempt to capture the State Committee of the MCP. The trooplift took seven hours; if the move had been made on foot it would have taken at least two days. No initial contact was made with the enemy, but on 25 May, as a result of fresh intelligence, a second trooplift was begun into a new area. Nine terrorists were killed and twelve of their camps destroyed. During the whole operation, which lasted a fortnight, the eight S-55s lifted a total of 1,623 troops and 35,000 lb. of stores on 415 sorties, while two Dragonflies carried out 94 reconnaissance and communications flights.

In October 1953, Operation VALIANT was mounted in an attempt to destroy the Central Politburo of the MCP and a number of terrorist camps which had been located in deep jungle in north-west Pahang. The operation involved four battalions of troops, and since movement on foot was virtually impossible helicopter transport was used extensively. The operation began with a trooplift of a battalion of 500 men into two small jungle landing zones, and companies of the remaining battalions were deployed and redeployed subsequently almost entirely by the S-55s. Over 2,700 troops were carried by helicopter in the operational area during October and November 1953, bringing the total for the year to almost 12,000 in 1,700 hours of flying by the S-55s of No 848 Squadron.

Because of the overworked state of No 848 Squadron's S-55s the unit's operational commitment was reduced in the early months of 1954. This, however, did not prevent the squadron from mounting a major effort in support of Operation TERMITE, the biggest combined operation of the Emergency, which unfolded in Perak from July 1954. The deployment of troops began in May, when the S-55s started flying men into landing zones prepared by the 22nd SAS Regiment. Between that month and September 1954, the S-55s of No 848 Squadron carried an average of 1,000 troops a month on a total of 2,448 sorties, most of which were of about forty minutes' duration.

In 1955, No 848 Squadron was joined in the trooplifting role by No 155 Squadron RAF, and the increase in the establishment of this unit to seventeen Whirlwinds, now suitably modified to be more effective as troop carriers, doubled the trooplifting capacity of the helicopter force in Malaya. In July 1955, the monthly total of troops lifted by helicopter rose to 3,461, the highest figure of the Emergency. Forty-three per cent of all troops positioned by helicopter in 1955 were flown in the S-55s of No 848 Squadron. In one notable operation during 1955, a complete battalion and two infantry companies – 600 men in all – were deployed in their operational areas by helicopter over a two-day period, having been assembled at Kluang by medium-range transport aircraft and rail transport.

In 1956, No 848 Squadron was redeployed to Sembawang for operations in Johore. A total of 25,700 troops were lifted by helicopter during the year, the main effort involving trooplifts in support of Operations LATIMER SOUTH and ENTER in north and north-east Negri Sembilan, HUCKSTER in the Kluang area of Johore and BONANZA in south Selangor. These operations resulted in the elimination of 150 terrorists in the closing months of the year and went on into 1957.

In December 1956, No 848 Squadron was withdrawn from operations in Malaya. During its four years in the theatre the squadron had transported over 45,000 troops and passengers. Part of the trooplifting commitment was now assumed by the Sycamores of No 194 Squadron, but the main effort was vested with the seventeen Whirlwinds of No 155 Squadron. Because of technical troubles, however, the Whirlwinds were grounded four times in the course of the year, including the whole of February, and trooplifts suffered accordingly, although from May onwards the monthly total of troops carried averaged 2,000. With both the Whirlwind and Sycamore forces beset by technical problems during 1958, it was only through the most careful husbanding of available helicopter resources that the trooplifting requirement could be met, although by this time there were fewer demands from the Security Forces.

Despite all the problems, the support helicopters did undertake one notable operation in 1958. In August, the 63rd and 99th Brigades launched a major offensive against the Regional Committee of the MCP in south Johore (Operation TIGER). During the early stage of this drive, the Whirlwind detachment at Seletar deployed 600 troops into the area, and a further 1,600 men were flown in during October. During this month 4,133 fully-equipped troops were flown into and out of jungle landing zones in north and south Malaya, a record for any single month of the campaign. About 60 per cent of these were deployed by Sycamores, which were now beginning to replace the Whirlwinds as a result of policy. In all, the Sycamores transported some 8,000 troops during 1958, about 30 per cent of the total.

In 1959, with No 155 Squadron being run down and the Sycamores of No 194 Squadron grounded in April, only five Whirlwinds of the newly-formed No 110 Squadron were available to carry out the remaining trooplifting commitments of the campaign, yet in October and November these carried over 1,600 troops in support of Operation BAMBOO in Perak, as well as maintaining their other transport commitments. The five Whirlwinds continued to carry 500 troops a month in the first half of 1960, mainly in support of the redeployment of the 1st Battalion The Royal Australian Regiment and the 1st Battalion 3rd East Anglian Regiment in the Operation BAMBOO area of Perak. Towards the end of the year, with the Emergency officially over, the Whirlwinds were transporting 600 troops a month in support of operations against terrorists in the Thailand border area.

During the Malayan campaign, helicopters, still at the experimental stage when they were introduced, carried 110,000 troops, and in the latter stages of the Emergency they were mainly responsible for carrying the war to the enemy in the deep jungle. The need for the medium helicopter in any future campaign of this nature had been clearly demonstrated.

In the trooplifting context, it is interesting to compare the experiences of the British forces in Malaya with those of the US forces in Korea. In that campaign the US Marine Corps employed transport helicopters from August 1951; these too were S-55s, designated HRS-1 in USMC service.

For the first five months of the war there were no US Army helicopters of any kind in Korea. The first to arrive, Sikorsky S-51s (H-5s), were pressed into service in the casualty evacuation role, and when General Matthew B. Ridgway assumed command of the UN forces in Korea in 1951 he followed the activities of the USMC rotary-wing transport unit with great interest. He was impressed by the cargo-carrying performance of the HRS-1 under all kinds of conditions, and in November 1951 he asked the Army Department to provide four helicopter transport battalions, each with twenty-eight helicopters. He pointed out that the events of the Korean War so far had proved conclusively that the Army vitally needed helicopters, and recommended that in the future each field army should be equipped with ten transport helicopter battalions. The Army Department agreed in principle to this recommendation, but was only willing to approve the assignment of four helicopter battalions to a field army.

By the end of 1951, the USMC HRS-1 helicopters had proved their worth so many times in the field that the arrival of the transport helicopters ordered by General Ridgway was awaited with great enthusiasm by the Army commanders. However, a heated argument on helicopter operations developed between Army and Air Force, both of whom were anxious to avoid duplication of the tasks to be carried out by their respective rotorcraft. Air transport within the combat zone, for example, was the Air Force's province, and a much closer definition of the Army's aims in this respect was needed. In the end, it was agreed that the Army helicopter units would be responsible for transporting Army supplies, equipment and personnel within the combat zone – an area defined as extending 50–100 miles behind the front line – but the Air Force would continue to airlift supplies, equipment and personnel into the combat zone from points outside.

In the event the argument turned out to be mainly academic, because it was not until March 1953 that the first Army transport helicopter unit arrived in Korea, and by that time the war was almost over.

CROP-SPRAYING OPERATIONS

One unique task carried out by the RAF and RN helicopters in Malaya was the spraying of terrorist cultivation plots in the jungle with toxic liquid. The first toxic liquid used was sodium arsenite; this proved effective, but it was poisonous to humans and the danger it posed to the native population was politically unacceptable. Eventually, it was replaced by a non-poisonous herbicide made up of a mixture of trioxene and diesolene, which killed all types of vegetation and made the ground unusable for a time.

The first such operation, using S-51s and S-55s, was mounted on 31 August 1953 after ten terrorist cultivations had been located by Austers of No 656 Squadron in the Kluang and Labis area of Johore. The cultivations were marked by the Austers, strafed by Hornets to eliminate any ground resistance, and then sprayed over a period of days by a pair of S-55s and an S-51. The operation, named CYCLONE I, was followed by another, CYCLONE II, and by the end of 1953 eighty-eight terrorist cultivations had been wiped out. Further crop-spraying operations were carried out during 1954, again with success, but after that they were abandoned because of a shortage of helicopters and reconnaissance aircraft. There was no doubt, however, that crop spraying was a significant factor in denying the terrorists vital food supplies, and in forcing them from their jungle hideouts and into contact with the Security Forces.

12

THE ROYAL MALAYAN AIR FORCE

The onset of the Malayan Emergency in 1948 created a serious gap in the Far Eastern theatre's air defences, because the only two squadrons with an air defence role, Nos 28 and 60, were now primarily engaged in anti-terrorist operations. In March 1949, at a meeting of the Air Council, plans were drawn up for the formation of three auxiliary fighter squadrons in Malaya, Singapore and Hong Kong. As well as providing a permanent air defence presence in the Far East if regular squadrons had to be withdrawn in the event of war, it was envisaged, with considerable forethought, that the auxiliary units would provide a firm base for the air forces which the Far Eastern colonies would need once they became independent.

The responsibility for forming the auxiliary squadrons initially rested with the colonial governments concerned. Operational control over them was to be vested in the local Air Officer Commanding, and the Air Ministry offered to provide aircraft and spares on free loan if the local governments would provide work services, freight charges and personnel costs. There was some delay while the governments of the Federation of Malaya and the Colony of Singapore were persuaded to pass the necessary legislation, but the ordinances establishing the Malayan Auxiliary Air Force (MAAF) were finally promulgated in May and June 1950.

The original scheme, which called for one auxiliary fighter squadron in Malaya and Singapore, was subsequently amended to provide four operational fighter squadrons in the Malayan theatre within four years of the formation of the MAAF. With the situation in Malaya growing worse, however, this period was reduced to two years.

Recruiting for the auxiliary squadrons that were to be based at Penang and Singapore began in May and June 1950, and a third squadron was formed at Kuala Lumpur in December 1951. Three associated fighter-control units were also in the process of formation, and plans were being made for the formation of another fighter squadron to be based on Singapore Island. The idea was that the MAAF squadrons were to gain initial flying experience on Tiger Moth and Auster light aircraft, then progress on to Harvards and surplus Spitfires before eventually receiving Vampire jet fighters. To this end the Penang, Singapore and Kuala Lumpur squadrons each received four Tiger Moths, followed by four Harvards in 1951 and 1952, and at the end of 1952 the Singapore squadron also received three Spitfires. The objective, prior to the receipt of jet fighters, was that each squadron would be established with eight Spitfires, plus two Harvards for training.

Progress in flying training, however, proved to be very slow, and in the summer of 1951 the Singapore squadron – the first to be formed – had only three pilots who were ready for conversion to Spitfires, four who were undergoing advanced training on Harvards and five basic training on Tiger Moths. In the Penang squadron, three pilots were training on Harvards and eight on Tiger Moths, with no progress being made at all towards conversion to Spitfires.

By March 1953 it was clear that none of the MAAF pilots under training would be ready to fly Vampires by the target date of 1954, even if the jet fighters became available and the governments of Malaya and Singapore were willing to finance their operation, and so the policy of providing auxiliary air defence squadrons was abandoned. It was agreed that the MAAF would eventually be replaced by a regular Malayan Air Force, and that in the interim the MAAF's light aircraft would be used for short-range transport and visual reconnaissance.

In 1953 the three squadrons of the MAAF were each equipped with four Tiger Moths and four Harvards, the three Spitfires of the Singapore squadron having been withdrawn. All three squadrons carried out occasional reconnaissance sorties and dropped leaflets over cultivation plots in southern Johore, Kedah and Negri Sembilan, but their effort was very limited; of the 20,000 reconnaissance sorties flown in support of Operation FIREDOG between January 1955 and July 1958, for example, the Singapore, Kuala Lumpur and Penang squadrons of the MAAF contributed only 86, 102 and 15 sorties respectively. By the end of this period each squadron was operating four de Havilland Chipmunk aircraft, replacing the worn-out Tiger Moths and Harvards.

In May 1958, a bill passed by the Federation of Malaya's Legislative Council established the Royal Malayan Air Force (RMAF), the MAAF's successor. This force was to consist of four Twin Pioneers, four single-engined Pioneers, four Chipmunks and 120 personnel, half of them seconded from the RAF. The RMAF was fully equipped by June 1959 and all its aircraft were based at Kuala Lumpur, alongside the remaining units of the FIREDOG Transport Support Force. On 1 July 1960 the Joint Operations Centre was handed over to the RMAF, which now assumed overall direction of flying in support of FIREDOG, and on 1 October 1960 the RAF station at Kuala Lumpur was also handed over.

The main task of the RMAF was to relieve the Commonwealth air forces of their commitment to supply the jungle forts that were manned by Federal Police units, but, because of a pilot shortage and servicing troubles with their Twin Pioneers, the RMAF had to be assisted in this task by the Pioneers of No 209 Squadron RAF for the first few months of 1960. The RMAF's first operational supply drop to a jungle fort was carried out in February 1960 from a Twin Pioneer, and from then until the end of the campaign in July RMAF Pioneers were occupied in transporting troops to jungle forts and dropping supplies and leaflets over northern Perak, the aircraft operating from an advanced base at Taiping.

13

PSYCHOLOGICAL WARFARE

The psychological warfare campaign that was waged in Malaya throughout the years of the Emergency had two main aims: to persuade the terrorists to surrender, disrupting their organization and spreading disaffection in the process, and to encourage the civilian population to oppose them.

At the start of the Emergency, information and directives to the population were disseminated through the Emergency Publicity Committee of the Department of Public Relations, but in June 1950 this task, as well as that of issuing anti-terrorist propaganda, was assumed by the Emergency Information Services at Federal Police Headquarters in Kuala Lumpur, with representatives at state or settlement and district levels. This was a logical step, because the main sources of information about terrorist locations and activities were police agents – usually former Communist supporters who still had contact with the terrorists – and members of the public who were known to be trustworthy in reporting suspicious movements to the police. Also, at an early stage in the campaign, the Police Special Branch knew the identities of all active CTs and their approximate spheres of operation.

In October 1952, with the psychological warfare campaign expanding, the Emergency Information Service was placed under the authority of the Director General of Information Services, and in March 1954 responsibility for the psychological offensive against the terrorists was placed under the control of the Psychological Warfare Section of the Director of Operations Staff, the Director of Information Services becoming responsible to the Home Affairs Department of the Government for disseminating Emergency propaganda and information to the public.

Information, propaganda and directives to the general public were disseminated by means of the whole media machinery: newspapers, posters, leaflets, press releases, touring loudspeaker vans, Radio Malaya broadcasts, films and voice broadcasts from loudspeaker-equipped aircraft. Some idea of the effort that went into the whole programme may be gleaned from the fact that the number of leaflets distributed by all methods rose from 30 million in 1948 to 53 million in 1950, to 77 million in 1953 and to an annual figure of over 100 million from 1954 to 1957. Also, the twelve mobile public address and cinema units that addressed one and a quarter million people in 1948 were expanded to a fleet of ninety-one units by 1953, and these addressed a monthly total of over one million people.

Some of the information passed to the general public by these means was relayed to terrorist groups in the jungle through Communist sympathizers, but for direct contact with the enemy the Psychological Warfare Department relied heavily on leaflet-dropping and voice-broadcast sorties by aircraft. In the beginning leaflet-dropping was the only method used, as voice-broadcast techniques from aircraft had yet to be developed. Some 100 leaflet-dropping sorties were flown during the first nine months of the campaign, mainly over Perak, southern Selangor and southern Johore; the leaflets dropped on these missions were primarily intended to advise the civilian population that a State of Emergency was in force. The aircraft used were mostly Dakotas of the medium-range transport force; these carried up to 800,000 leaflets which were despatched from the aircraft in bundles of 5,000 by personnel of No 55 Air Despatch Company of the RASC. Using this method, a good distribution of leaflets over an area 1,000 yards square could be achieved. Drops of smaller numbers of leaflets on to pinpoint targets were usually made by Auster observation aircraft of No 656 Squadron, which were under the operational control of the Army formations to which the various flights were attached.

Leaflet-dropping operations intensified after April 1949, with an average of ten monthly sorties being flown until December 1950. In the course of 229 sorties during this period more than 12.5 million leaflets were dropped, one million of them on known terrorist concentrations to announce the terms of surrender which were promulgated in September 1949. The effort was stepped up even further in 1951, many leaflets carrying information on rewards for informers. The peak month was in June 1951, when 2.25 million leaflets were dropped on 106 sorties, mostly in support of anti-terrorist operations in Johore. To meet the enhanced requirement, the Dakotas and Valettas of the medium-range transport force were assisted by bombers of the offensive support force, which dropped leaflets after air strikes.

During 1952 the brunt of the leaflet-dropping effort was borne by the Valettas of No 52 Squadron, which during one period of intensive flying in August dropped 3,276,000 leaflets. By the end of the year, there was considerable evidence from surrendered terrorists that the propaganda campaign was having a major effect, and in 1953 the leaflet-dropping effort was stepped up from an average of eleven sorties a month in the first half of the year to twenty-three in the second half. Over 60 million leaflets were dropped in the course of the year, with the maximum effort in October, when 19,536,000 leaflets were dropped. Fifteen million of these contained a message from a high-ranking terrorist officer who had surrendered; these were dropped by the Lincoln bombers of No 1 Squadron RAAF and No 83 Squadron RAF, the latter on temporary deployment from Hemswell in the United Kingdom.

The psychological warfare campaign reached its peak in 1955, when 141 million leaflets were dropped on 365 sorties. The week following 9 September 1955, when an amnesty was declared, saw the biggest leaflet-dropping operations of the entire Emergency; in seven days, Valettas dropped 21 million leaflets over the jungle, setting out the surrender terms, while a further 6 million leaflets carried information on surrender points and 'safe areas'. Following this short period of intense activity, and with peace talks appearing to be a valid prospect, all forms of anti-terrorist propaganda were curtailed and the number of leaflets dropped fell from 29 million in September 1955 to less than 5 million in each of the last three months of the year.

The leaflet-dropping operations were once again stepped up in 1956, when it became clear that the peace talks were abortive, and 100 million leaflets were dropped in the course of the year by the Valettas of Nos 48, 52 and 110 Squadrons, the Bristol Freighters of No 41 (RNZAF) Squadron and the Austers of No 656 Squadron. In the following year the number of leaflet-dropping sorties showed a steady decrease, for the reason that the number of terrorists remaining in the jungle was dwindling. The most intensive flying period of the year occurred between 7 and 9 September, when Valettas of the air-transport support force at Kuala Lumpur dropped 8,320,000 leaflets and the Austers of No 656 Squadron a further 3.6 million, the leaflets setting out the terms of a new surrender agreement which was to remain in force until the end of the year. This operation, GREENLAND I, was followed by a second, GREENLAND II, when nearly 13 million leaflets were dropped between 17 and 21 December 1957, the latest peace offer having now been extended to 30 April 1958.

In the early months of 1958 terrorists were surrendering in growing numbers, and the success of the psychological warfare campaign led to the extension of the surrender deadline until 31 July, a further 8.5 million leaflets being dropped in GREENLAND III. At the same time, 2.5 million leaflets were dropped regularly each month as part of the general anti-communist propaganda offensive.

Leaflet-dropping continued for some time after the Emergency had been officially declared over, and nearly one and a half million leaflets were still being delivered from the air each month at the end of 1960. The total of leaflets dropped during the entire Malayan campaign reached 500 million, in the course of 2,500 sorties.

Leaflet-dropping operations were closely linked with voice broadcasts from early 1953, trials having been carried out in airborne loudhailing techniques from October 1952 with a loudspeaker-equipped C-47 borrowed from the USAF at the request of General Templer, the Director of Operations. Two Valettas of Headquarters FEAF were initially equipped with voice-broadcasting systems, but their engine noise was found to be excessive and they were replaced by Dakotas. The first of these, borrowed from the RAAF and fitted with broadcasting equipment from one of the Valettas, operated alongside the other Valetta until 23 February 1954, when the Valetta crashed on Mount Ophir (4,187 feet high) in Johore with the total loss of the aircraft and all on board.

Demands for so-called 'Voice' aircraft were increasing, and it was decided to form a Voice Aircraft Flight. This became 'C' Flight of No 267 Squadron, which was based at Kuala Lumpur. The flight was established with three Dakotas and two Auster aircraft (broadcast trials by an Auster had been made in January 1954, and had proved very satisfactory, the loudhailing being carried out from a height of 1,500 feet at 42 knots).

The Voice Aircraft Flight's first RAF Dakota, flown out from the United Kingdom, arrived on 12 June 1954 and was made ready for operations by the 23rd, when the RAAF Dakota returned to Australia. A second Dakota arrived on 13 July 1954, followed by a third in January 1955, when the Voice Flight attained its maximum establishment of three Dakotas and two Austers.

In November 1958, No 267 Squadron changed its numberplate to No 209. The Voice Flight continued to operate from Kuala Lumpur until January 1959 when, because of the elimination of CTs and the declaration of 'White Areas' in the southern part of Malaya, it was decided that the Voice Flight would be moved to Penang in order to be nearer to the remaining 'Black Areas' of northern Malaya. Because of the often dangerous flying conditions in this area, and the hazards of the mountainous terrain, the two Austers were withdrawn at this point. On 26 January 1959, the flight suffered a serious loss when one of the Dakotas crashed on take-off from Kuala Lumpur and was totally destroyed. In November 1959, with the move of No 209 Squadron to Seletar, on Singapore Island, the Voice Flight was transferred to No 52 Squadron at Kuala Lumpur, the flight remaining as a detachment at Penang.

To achieve the maximum psychological effect on the CTs, following an encounter with the Security Forces, Voice Aircraft were used with the minimum amount of delay, in order to take advantage of low CT morale and exploit any setbacks the terrorists may have suffered, with promises of fair treatment to all who decided to 'self-renew' (the term 'surrender' was never used, as this would have meant unacceptable loss of face). The text of the broadcast was of primary importance, and certain strict rules had to be followed.

Most importantly, all statements had to be true. This principle was rigidly adhered to in Malaya, and it was noticeable in statements by surrendered terrorists that they never doubted the information delivered by Voice Aircraft. Threats were not used unless the authorities intended to carry out the threatened action and were capable of doing so. The messages had to be brief and clear, with words and phrases carefully chosen. Six or seven short sentences were first drafted in English, translated into the required language, and finally recorded in the correct dialect. The recordings were usually made in the studios of Radio Malaya under ideal conditions, although recordings were sometimes made to a high standard in the Voice Flight office using an acoustic booth or, in an emergency, on board the Dakota itself.

The Voice Dakotas were equipped with a large diesel generator, installed in the fuselage, which produced 230 volts. The tape-recorder used a special cassette carrying 19 feet of tape, the two ends being spliced together to form an endless repeatable tape. On operational tapes the recorded message ran for twenty-seven seconds, followed by a three-second pause before being repeated. The message was amplified by four amplifiers, each of which delivered an output of 500 watts to the speakers. The latter were mounted on a jettisonable boom slung under the aircraft at an angle of 45 degrees to the vertical, and directed towards the port side. The quality of the broadcast and the correct functioning of the equipment were constantly monitored by the tannoy operator, seated at a control station by the main door; he was also responsible for changing tapes into different languages and dialects at the request of the aircraft captain.

Loudhailing operations required very precise flying and were sometimes dangerous, since the Dakota had to be held at a speed of 70 knots, which was very close to the stall – a hazardous occupation in the turbulence of the Malayan mountains. Straight-line flying in squares, with all turns to the left and working towards the centre at 2,000-yard intervals produced the best results, since the speakers covered an area of 2,000 yards to the left of the aircraft and 500 yards to the right, from an optimum height of 2,500 feet above the ground. For a broadcast to a small target, or village, an orbiting technique would be used to give continuous ground reception.

By the end of 1956 the Voice Flight aircraft were flying an average of seventy-five sorties a month. Much of the loudhailing was concerned with the tactical exploitation of specific terrorist eliminations, such as the killing of Ah Hoi, the South Malayan Bureau Representative and State Committee Secretary of the MCP in Negri Sembilan, on 11 October 1956. From 1957, however, the number of loudhailing sorties flown by the Dakotas was gradually reduced in order to conserve the limited flying time that was left to the ageing aircraft.

Overall, the psychological warfare campaign was very successful and a key factor in bringing the Emergency to an end. During the first two months of Voice Flight operations in 1953, eight terrorists surrendered as a result of hearing aerial broadcasts and others claimed to have been partly persuaded by them. By 1955, 70 per cent of all surrendered terrorists who had heard an aerial broadcast stated that it had influenced their decision to give themselves up, and in many cases it had been the major factor involved. The statement of one surrendered terrorist alone remains a testimony to the effectiveness of the leaflet-dropping and loudhailing campaign in encouraging defection from the Communist cause:

> 'After the attack on our cultivation area we fled to another area where we saw many Government propaganda leaflets and safe-conduct passes. I picked up some of the leaflets intending to use them when coming out to surrender. A few days later we heard voices coming from an aeroplane calling on us all to surrender and offering good treatment. We all agreed to this suggestion.'

14

THE MALAYAN EMERGENCY: CONCLUSIONS

The achievements of the Malayan Races' Liberation Army during the period of the Emergency should not be underestimated. Insurgent strength never rose much above 6,000 and they never had any significant external help, and yet at the peak of the Emergency their activities were tying down some 300,000 Security Forces personnel – regular troops, police and home guard. Between June 1948 and Independence Day on 31 August 1957, the Security Forces killed and captured 7,643 terrorists and persuaded 1,938 more to surrender; but the Security Forces themselves lost 1,851 killed and 2,526 wounded, figures that include 1,000 police and 500 British and Commonwealth troops killed. In addition, the terrorists killed 2,473 civilians during the whole of the Emergency and wounded 1,385, with a further 810 missing. The cost of the anti-terrorist campaign was enormous, too; from 1948 until Malayan Independence in 1957 it has been estimated that the total expenditure was more than £700 million, of which £525 million was provided by the United Kingdom.

At first, everything seemed to be on the side of the terrorists. They organized their hit-and-run raids from camps hidden in the jungle, well-screened from the air, with sentries out to half a mile and escape routes well worked out. The Min Yuen organization brought them tens of thousands of sympathizers from the Chinese element of the population and guaranteed the supply of money, food, medicine and intelligence. The terrorists forced rubber estates, tin mines, police stations and isolated homes to become armed camps surrounded by high wire fences, lit at night by searchlights and patrolled constantly by guards. Planters and miners slept with revolvers under their pillows, with grenades on nearby tables. Bedrooms became strongpoints, with Bren guns sited at windows. People travelled in lorries converted into armoured trucks, with escorts. No stretch of the road could be guaranteed safe from ambush, and railway travellers had to contend with derailment as a permanent hazard along isolated stretches of track.

Yet the Communists did not win their insurgent war in Malaya. They could never have won. Their initial successes were mainly achieved as a result of the slow British response to events, and gave an illusory indication of their strength, even though the damage they inflicted on the rubber and tin industries, only just beginning to recover from the effects of the Japanese occupation, brought development to a virtual standstill for three years and posed a very real threat to the security and economy of the Federation.

It was only with the appointment of Lieutenant-General Sir Harold Briggs as Director of Operations in March 1950 that a true military response to the Communist threat was initiated, and then the severe disadvantages under which the Communists were operating began to appear. First of all, it soon became clear that the Communist Terrorist Organization (CTO) had seriously miscalculated the support they were likely to get from the two and a half million Chinese in Malaya. There was no rush to join the ranks of the MRLA in the jungle. Also, the Government policy of grouping Chinese elements into settlements where they could be effectively controlled and protected paid early dividends; with security came loyalty, brought about partly by effective government and partly by an intensive propaganda campaign, and once this had been guaranteed the Security Forces could devote their full attention to eliminating the insurgents.

The CTO failed to realize at first that to terrorize the 'imperialists' and their economic organizations brought immense hardship to the workers and peasants, the very people who, according to Mao, should have been readily won over to the Communist cause. Instead of ensuring overall sympathy, the most they obtained from towns and villages was grudging and fearful co-operation. Their plans to establish liberated areas also collapsed when the estate owners failed to flee and instead set about building up their own defence forces, composed of workers who remained remarkably loyal unless they were terrorized. By the time the terrorists realized their mistake and revised their policy, it was too late. The New Village scheme to resettle half a million Chinese squatters – the 'sea of the people in which the guerrillas aimed to swim like fish', to use Mao's description – had been firmly implemented and the 'sea' no longer existed.

To counter Communist efforts to re-establish supply lines, stringent Government controls were imposed on the sale and movement of essential commodities, especially food. Shopkeepers were made to keep records of sales, farmers had to record their harvests, villages and estates became guarded larders. It was clearly stated that the Emergency would not be permitted to hold up economic and political progress; in April 1951, Sir Henry Gurney gave political and community leaders ministerial status and entrusted them with the control of some Government departments. Even when the Emergency was at its most critical point, Malayans were taking steps towards self-government.

The clear message was that Britain would keep her promise to see the Federation achieve independence, and that message was repeated with even greater emphasis by General Templer. The end result was to deprive the Communists of one of their strongest propaganda weapons – that Britain was essentially an imperialist power interested only in preserving her hold over Malaya.

On the military front, the Communists had seriously underestimated the ability of Commonwealth forces to adapt themselves to jungle warfare. Those of the CTO who had belonged to the Malayan People's Anti-Japanese Army had seen British and Australian troops suffer early defeat; had they been able to witness soldiers of those same armies in action in Burma and New Guinea later in the war, their outlook might have been very different. Admittedly, operations during the Emergency involving large numbers of troops met with little success, but when hunter-killer platoons were built up, composed of tough, aggressive soldiers well-trained in jungle warfare and marksmanship, acting on information supplied by an increasingly efficient Police Special Branch intelligence service and assisted by Dayak trackers from Sarawak, the story changed. These troops outfought the terrorists on their own ground and, with substantial air support, ensured that the jungle was no longer a safe refuge. It is a fact that troops already acclimatized to jungle warfare produced the best results in the anti-terrorist campaign; although Gurkha troops accounted for more terrorists killed than any others, because of the length of time their units spent on active service in Malaya, achieving an average of one kill per contact between 1953 and 1955, they were beaten during that same period by the East Africans, who averaged 1.13 kills per contact, followed by the British and Malays with an average of 1.00 and 0.68 kills per contact.

Perhaps the biggest mistake of all made by the Communists in Malaya was to believe that they could emulate the achievements of the Vietminh guerrillas in Indo-China, who by 1948 were locked in a deadly war with the French colonial authorities. The Vietminh, under the leader Ho Chi Minh and his able military commander, General Giap, were already strong and well-armed, and were conducting their operations from a near-impregnable mountain fortress. For a time there was stalemate, but Ho Chi Minh, while sustaining intense political pressure and launching raids on French border garrisons, set about reorganizing his army on a regular basis, and when Mao Zedong's victory over Chiang Kai-shek in China brought the Chinese Communist forces to the frontier of Indo-China, the Vietminh found themselves with a secure base for rest and re-training, a source of ammunition, equipment and instructors. By 1950 Ho Chi Minh possessed thirty regular battalions in the north of the country, with a large number of guerrilla units operating in the south.

The CTO in Malaya had no such friendly cross-border sanctuary, nor did they have an external source of modern arms and equipment. There is no parallel between the terrorist campaign in Malaya and the efficient, well-organized war waged by Ho Chi Minh. Nor is there any parallel between the British administration in Malaya and the oppressive, heavy-handed attitude of the French colonial power in Indo-China, with its belief in the use of extreme military force to keep a restless population in check.

In a sense, the Communists in Malaya elected to fight the wrong war in the wrong place, not least because over half the population were Muslim Malays for whom Communism had little appeal. They seriously miscalculated the strength of their position, their chances of support from Russia and China, and the British response. Their leadership was poor, their communications easily disrupted, and their application of Maoist strategy a failure. Even so, it took a force outnumbering them sometimes by fifty to one, itself applying Maoist principles, efficient, with huge reserves, to defeat them; and yet they never surrendered.

The Malayan Emergency holds many lessons on how an anti-guerrilla campaign can be effectively conducted. It also indicates how effective Maoist strategy can be if properly applied under favourable conditions.

Those conditions might have been favourable if the population of Malaya had been starving, or oppressed, or suffering under a corrupt regime. None of these factors applied, and the peoples of Malaya soon came to realize – even those who had initially wavered – that what they had already was infinitely better than anything Communism had to offer them. They were the real victors.

15

CONFRONTATION

In the closing months of 1962, preparations were well-advanced under Great Britain's sponsorship to incorporate British North Borneo and Singapore Island into the concept of a Greater Malaysia, the aim being to bring a greater degree of independence to the remaining British territories in South-East Asia while retaining them within the British Commonwealth.

This concept aroused fierce opposition from the Republic of Indonesia, whose President Soekarno had dreamed since his accession in 1945 of bringing the Malay Peninsula, Singapore, Sarawak, Sabah and Brunei under the domination of a Greater Indonesia. The focal point of Soekarno's hostility lay in Borneo, and it was in this large and underdeveloped island that the first signs of what was later to be termed 'Confrontation' first became manifest late in 1962.

Borneo is one of the largest islands in the world, measuring about 800 miles from north to south and 600 miles at its widest point from east to west. It is mostly covered in dense jungle and the interior is sparsely populated, most of the population centres lying on the coastal fringes. Its climate is similar to that of Malaya except that the rainfall is heavier and more frequent. The main features of the island are heat and humidity, with temperatures in the middle to high eighties Fahrenheit. It is a very oppressive and exhausting climate for Europeans to work, let alone fight, in, and this fact must be borne in mind when examining the achievements of the Commonwealth forces that were committed to security operations there during the period of the Confrontation.

In 1962 Borneo was divided into four states. The largest of these was Kalimantan, an undeveloped tract of jungle covering three-quarters of the island. Until 1949 Kalimantan formed part of the Netherlands East Indies, but had been ceded to Indonesia when the latter gained independence. The second largest state, which was also undeveloped, was Sarawak, with its capital at Kuching. For administrative purposes Sarawak was split up into five divisions, the First Division being the southernmost and centred on the capital. The interior of Sarawak was

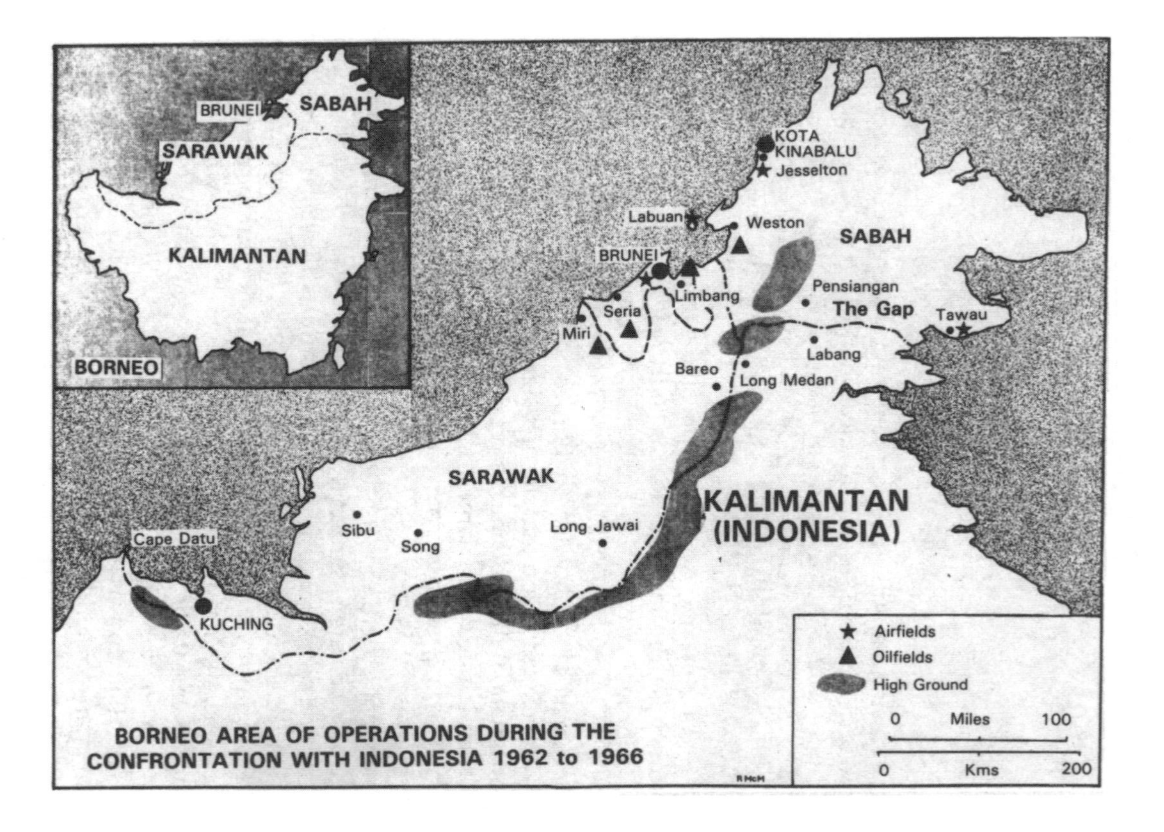

BORNEO AREA OF OPERATIONS DURING THE CONFRONTATION WITH INDONESIA 1962 to 1966

inhabited by the Ibans, tribesmen who lived in communal long houses and who were the original Borneo head-hunters.

To the north of Sarawak lay Sabah, or North Borneo, with its capital at Jesselton on the coast. It also had a port, Tawau, on the east coast. Together, Sabah and Sarawak formed the original Crown Colony of North Borneo. Finally, sandwiched between Sabah and Sarawak, was the small, independent and extremely wealthy state of Brunei, which derived its income from the oilfields at Seria and which was ruled by a Sultan.

The frontier between Kalimantan and the three British-supported territories was some 900 miles long, most of it enveloped in dense jungle. The border could therefore be infiltrated fairly easily at almost any point, provided the infiltrators could penetrate the jungle in the first place. Although the coastal fringes were relatively flat, there were rugged and mountainous regions in the interior, with peaks rising to 13,000 feet and frequently shrouded in mist and low cloud.

Revolutionary factions, supported by Indonesia and collectively styling themselves the North Kalimantan National Army, had been engaged in covert subversion in the three Borneo territories for some time, and in June 1962 the British Resident in the Fifth Division of Sarawak had warned the authorities in Kuching of growing political intrigue. On 7 December the Commissioner-General for South-East Asia, who had been visiting Brunei, informed the Commander-in-Chief in Singapore that a rebel attack on either the Sarawak oilfield at Miri or the Brunei oilfield was a distinct possibility on the following day. Plans already existed to airlift an infantry company from Singapore to reinforce the Brunei police in the event of an emergency, and accordingly a company of the 1/2nd Gurkhas was brought to readiness, together with its tactical headquarters.

On 8 December 1962, a revolt by the North Kalimantan National Army (NKNA) broke out as predicted, not only in Brunei but also in the Fourth and Fifth Divisions of Sarawak. The rebel forces involved, led by a 34-year-old absentee politician named A. M. Azahari, were reported to comprise fifteen companies, each of 150 men, armed with shotguns, parangs, axes and spears. Their targets were mainly police stations, several of which were taken by surprise and overwhelmed.

At this time the Far East Air Force had a considerable number of transport aircraft at its disposal. Twelve Hastings of No 48 Squadron, four Beverleys of No 34 Squadron, some Pioneers of No 209 Squadron and a Britannia of RAF Transport Command, flying on scheduled routes from the United Kingdom, were immediately assigned to airlifting the emergency force, which had now been increased to two companies of the 1/2nd Gurkhas. The Britannia flew to the island of Labuan, some twenty miles off the coast of Sabah, which the RAF used as a staging post and which had a permanent runway, while the Beverleys and Pioneers flew into Brunei civil airfield. Attempts had been made to obstruct the latter, but the obstacles had been removed by the Controller of Civil Aviation and members of the local fire brigade. The airfield was secured by the first load of Gurkhas, ninety-three troops in all.

The situation that met the reinforcement troops deployed in Brunei was confused. In the town itself the rebels had been driven out of the power station, which they had captured earlier in the day, and attacks on the main police station, the Sultan's palace and the Prime Minister's residence had all been repulsed by police with the help of a platoon of the North Borneo Field Force, the latter having been ferried from Jesselton in a Twin Pioneer of No 209 Squadron and various light aircraft.

Elsewhere, at Tutong and Muara, the unprotected police stations had been captured by the rebels, who were in control of the towns. The police station at the important Seria oilfield was also in rebel hands. The situation here was serious, because the rebels had forty-eight European hostages and had used them as shields in an attack on Panaga police station, at the western edge of the oilfield. The attack was repulsed, but in the exchange of fire one hostage was killed and five wounded.

Later in the day the police post at Anduki and its adjacent airfield were captured by the rebels, who at once used vehicles to obstruct the airstrip. By mid-afternoon on 8 December, therefore, virtually the whole of Brunei was in rebel hands with the exception of Brunei town itself. In Sarawak, rebel forces seized the town of Limbang for a period, but were driven out by police reinforcements and the situation restored by 06.30 hours on the following morning.

By dawn on 9 December, a tactical headquarters had been set up in Brunei town police station under Major Lloyd Williams and patrols of Gurkhas were being sent out. The Force Commander decided to give immediate priority to the relief of Seria and the recapture of Anduki airstrip; both places were reconnoitred by a Twin Pioneer of No 209 Squadron, carrying the Force Commander and the Brunei Police Commissioner. As a result of this, plans were made to land troops simultaneously at both objectives, even though rebel flags were seen to be flying over most of the area.

The troops earmarked for the operation practised rapid deplaning and were transported to the target area in five Twin Pioneers of No 209 Squadron, carrying a total of 60 men, and a Beverley of No 34 Squadron with 110 men. The Pioneers landed on a grassy area of soft ground to the west of the Seria oilfield, their wingtips literally brushing through tree branches as they approached to land, while the Beverley made a short landing at Anduki. Its 110 troops made their exit in full battle order and the aircraft took off one minute and forty-eight seconds after landing, sustaining two hits in the rear fuselage and tail unit from rebel automatic gunfire.

Shortly before the troops flew into the area, the rebels holding Seria had telephoned the Shell Petroleum Company with a threat to use the hostages again as a screen in a further attack on Panaga police station. A Canberra of No 45 Squadron, normally based at Tengah but now detached to Labuan, was summoned and made a series of dummy attacks on the rebel-held police post, bringing a promise from the rebels that the hostages would not be harmed.

On 11 December the Pioneers and Beverleys flew more reinforcement into Anduki in torrential rain. The insurgents at Anduki had now been forced to surrender and Army units closed in on Seria, an attack on this police post being planned for the 13th. In preparation for this, four Hawker Hunter FGA.9 fighter-bombers were deployed from Tengah to Labuan, and prior to the attack all four made a simulated strike on the police station, one of them firing its cannon over the roof and into the sea. This was followed by a broadcast from a loudspeaker-equipped Pioneer of No 209 Squadron, urging the rebels to surrender. Immediately after the broadcast the police station was stormed by Gurkha troops, who rescued all the hostages. After this successful assault rebel morale fell rapidly and other centres were quickly recaptured by a Royal Marine Commando and other reinforcements brought in by sea.

The Commando involved was No 42, which had been flown to Labuan Island and then ferried to Brunei town to relieve the hard-pressed Gurkhas. L Company of No 42 Commando was assigned the task of releasing the British Resident, his wife and several other Europeans from Limbang, twelve miles up-river, where the rebels were holding them. With the help of the crews of two naval minesweepers, HMS *Fiskerton* and HMS *Chawton*, the Commandos acquired two old Z lighters, which were quickly serviced and fortified. The company commander was briefed and the small force set out at midnight on 11/12 December along the narrow river covered in mangrove swamp and barely negotiable in places.

After laying up silently when just in sight of Limbang, the two craft, with Vickers medium machine-guns mounted in their open bows, moved off slowly at 05.00. As they were approaching what appeared to be a sleepy village they suddenly came under heavy fire. The Commandos disembarked and, still under fire, made a frontal assault on the village. After an hour's firefight the rebels were driven off or taken prisoner, and the hostages, two of whom had been threatened with execution at dawn, were released unharmed.

Meanwhile, No 40 Commando had been on exercise aboard HMS *Albion* off Mombasa when the aircraft carrier was ordered east with all speed. At Singapore, she embarked Headquarters 3 Commando Brigade and sailed for Labuan. No 40 Commando were landed by helicopter and coastal craft at Kuching, from where they were transported by air to join up with No 42 Commando on their jungle patrols. Other British warships, including HMS *Bulwark*, HMS *Tiger*, destroyers and frigates, minesweepers and tank-landing craft, were despatched to the trouble spot by the Commander-in-Chief Far East, bringing more troops from Singapore and heavier fire support.

Within a week the main insurgent forces had been broken up and dispersed, but operations continued to round up those who had fled to jungle hideouts. While helicopters from the Commando ships supported the troops, supplying rations and other necessities and evacuating casualties and prisoners, coastal minesweepers maintained sea and river patrols, watching out for pirates, smugglers and illegal immigrants. When abnormally bad weather brought torrential rain that swept away houses and destroyed livestock and crops, the Westland Wessex helicopters of Nos 845, 846 and 848 Squadrons carried food and supplies to cut-off villages.

By February 1963 all major towns in Sarawak and Brunei had been cleared of rebel activities, and life was beginning to return to normal. British casualties during the anti-rebel operations had amounted to seven killed, five of them Royal Marines, and twenty-eight wounded. Between sixty and seventy rebels had been killed and ten times that number wounded. The North Kalimantan National Army and its associated political arm, the Brunei People's Party, were banned and several key figures arrested. Its leader fled to the Philippines.

Although the initial, localized revolt had been crushed, it signalled a steady increase in raids from across the border in Kalimantan. The 1,000-mile frontier was patrolled by Gurkhas, Royal Marines of Nos 40 and 42 Commandos (the aircraft carrier HMS *Albion* being used as a floating base for both RM and military personnel during these operations, the patrols being ferried to and from their operational areas by Wessex helicopters of Nos 845, 846 and 848 Squadrons) and by A Squadron of the 22nd Special Air Service Regiment, but the screening was inevitably thin, and on 12 April 1963 a platoon of Indonesian troops crossed the border and attacked a police station at Tebedu in the First Division of Sarawak. The raid was repulsed with little difficulty and the Indonesians retreated across the frontier, two miles away, when reinforcements arrived in the shape of armoured cars of the Queen's Royal Irish Hussars and 1 Troop of A Squadron 22nd SAS. A second raid, on a police post at Seng, was also beaten off in August.

Then, on 28 September, the Indonesians scored their first major success when 200 troops attacked a small outpost at Long Jawai in the Third Division of Sarawak. The garrison there consisted of six Gurkha soldiers, three policemen and twenty-one Border Scouts, who put up a spirited defence but who were eventually overwhelmed. However, Long

Jawai lay some 50 miles inside Sarawak, and the Indonesians had to get back to the border on foot and by river boat, which proved to be their downfall. Platoons of the 1st Battalion 2nd Gurkha Rifles were quickly deployed by the Wessex helicopters of No 845 Squadron to ambush positions along the Indonesians' line of retreat. During the next twelve days the Indonesian raiding force sustained very heavy casualties. In one spectacularly successful ambush, twenty-six of the raiders were killed in their river boats by a Gurkha platoon.

By this time Malaysia had come into existence, on 16 September 1963, and the British Government had made it plain that it would do everything in its power to support Greater Malaysia. Indonesia, for its part, had broken off diplomatic relations with the new state, and the raid on Long Jawai was a clear indication that the Indonesians intended to resort to the increased use of force in an attempt to establish their claim to the territories of northern Borneo. Incursions by bands of guerrillas from across the Kalimantan border were stepped up in the closing weeks of 1963; most of these bands comprised local Kalimantan Indonesians, with a proportion of Sarawak Chinese, about 1,500 of whom had been trained in Kalimantan with the primary object of terrorizing the local people in order to prevent them from supporting the Security Forces. In many ways, the tactics used were a carbon copy of those employed by the Communist terrorists in Malaya in the early years of the Emergency.

Late in December 1963, a strong force of raiders, including about thirty-five regular Indonesian troops – later identified as Marines – crossed the border near Tawau on the north-east coast of Sabah, their objective being to capture the village of Kalabatan 30 miles west of Tawau. The raiding force attacked the village just before midnight, taking a half company of the 3rd Royal Malay Regiment completely by surprise. The company commander and seven soldiers were killed and nineteen wounded. Major-General Walter Walker CBE DSO, the Director of Operations in Borneo, rapidly deployed platoons of the 1/10th Gurkha Rifles by helicopter along the raiders' line of retreat, using the same tactics he had employed after the attack on Long Jawai. Within a month, all but six of the raiding force had been killed or captured.

In January 1964 the Security Forces registered another success when a small patrol of the 1st Battalion The Royal Leicestershire Regiment attacked an Indonesian camp on the Sarawak–Sabah border. The Indonesians fled, leaving seven dead and large quantities of arms and ammunition.

During the closing months of 1963, the helicopter squadrons of the Royal Navy and the RAF (Nos 66, 103 and 110) had maintained a heavy programme of ferrying, air supply, casualty evacuation and search-and-rescue among the units deployed along the frontier. The RAF squadrons, based in Singapore, deployed detachments at Kuching and their workload was extremely heavy, so the arrival of reinforcements from the United Kingdom in December 1963 was greeted with some relief. These reinforcements, codenamed SPINEFORCE, comprised the Whirlwind Mk 10 helicopters of No 225 Squadron and four twin-rotor Westland Belvederes of No 26 Squadron. They had been taking part in an exercise in the Middle East when they were directed to Kuching, arriving by sea. Their presence meant that the transport helicopter force available to General Walker was virtually doubled.

Unlike the situation that had existed in Malaya during the Emergency, the Security Forces engaged in the confrontation in Borneo had to take into account the threat of offensive action by aircraft of the Indonesian Air Force (AURI). Late in 1963 AURI aircraft made several infringements of Malaysian airspace; these were mostly B-25 Mitchell bombers escorted by F-51 Mustang fighters, both of Second World War vintage, but AURI had a much more modern combat potential in the shape of Russian-built MiG-17 jet fighters and Il-28 jet bombers. More serious still, Indonesia had recently acquired a number of Tupolev Tu-16 Badger medium jet bombers, and her transport force had been augmented by a delivery of several Lockheed C-130 Hercules from the United States.

Nine overflights of Sarawak and Sabah were reported in December 1963 and incursions continued early in 1964, despite a ceasefire negotiated in Bangkok (which turned out to be completely ineffectual), the Indonesian Government now making public its intention to supply the guerrilla forces by air. Between 31 January and 2 February 1964, various AURI aircraft dropped propaganda leaflets by day and night over widely scattered areas of the North Borneo states, ranging from Kuching in the west to Tawau in the east. Drops made at points near the border were made by B-25s, C-47 Dakotas and C-130s, and night leaflet drops were made at points deeper inside Malaysian territory. In the early hours of 2 February, heavy jet aircraft were reported to have been heard in areas where leaflets were found later that day.

As a result of these operations, HQ Far East Air Force decided as a matter of necessity to establish an Air Defence Identification Zone (ADIZ) around the borders of Sabah and Sarawak, extending to three miles offshore. To police the ADIZ, No 20 Squadron, based at Tengah, deployed eight Hunter FGA.9 fighters to Borneo on 20 February 1964, four aircraft positioning at Labuan and four at Kuching. In addition, four Gloster Javelin Mk 9R aircraft of No 60 Squadron were deployed at each of these airfields, so providing eastern Malaysia with a permanent day-and-night, all-weather air defence system. The Mk 9R version of the Javelin had provision for underwing fuel tanks, resulting in a useful increase in its endurance; most important of all, its Firestreak air-to-air missile armament, combined with its four 30 mm guns, made it a formidable adversary.

The Rules of Engagement applying to interceptions were amended to give pilots the authority to engage and destroy Indonesian aircraft overflying the ADIZ without first having to obtain authority from the ground. The overall result of the fighter deployment was that incursions declined markedly in the early weeks of 1964, and guerrilla raids across the border from Kalimantan were undertaken without any form of Indonesian air support. The RAF air defences were frequently augmented by the deployment of a fleet carrier to the area. The carriers *Centaur, Victorious, Eagle* and *Ark Royal* were all stationed in Malaysian waters at some time during the period of confrontation, with their squadrons of Hawker Siddeley Sea Vixen fighters and Blackburn Buccaneer strike aircraft.

Another important RAF contribution throughout the confrontation was made by the Canberra PR.7s of No 81 Squadron. Vast areas of Borneo were virtually unmapped, which was a great hindrance to ground operations. No 81 Squadron deployed Canberras at Labuan and from there they flew lengthy sorties along the frontier, providing complete photo-mapping coverage and producing prints of a quality that clearly showed frontier crossing points, jungle tracks and isolated long houses. The Canberra's endurance enabled it to cover a lot of ground in a single sortie, and its high speed ensured the minimum delay in processing the results and producing the large-scale tactical maps which the Security Forces badly needed.

In March 1964, after a lull, the Indonesians resumed their infiltration activities, and now the Security Forces began to encounter regular Indonesian troops in increasing numbers. On 7 March, a platoon of the 2/10th Gurkhas was called upon to dislodge an Indonesian force from a strong position on a pinnacle on the border of Sarawak's Second Division. Two Gurkha soldiers were killed during the approach, and it was only after a stiff firefight that the Indonesians withdrew, leaving behind one dead man. Intelligence later confirmed that he was one of a forty-strong unit of the 328th Raider Battalion. Some days later the Indonesians returned to the same ridge, but about 16 miles to the east. On this occasion their position was attacked by two Wessex helicopters firing SS11 wire-guided anti-tank missiles, a troop of 105 mm artillery and two Saladin armoured cars, but even then the Gurkhas had a stiff fight before they were able to dislodge the enemy, who left two dead soldiers behind when they withdrew.

In the weeks that followed there was a further lull in large-scale Indonesian raiding across the border. Following a period of intense diplomatic activity, a high-level conference had been arranged to take place in Tokyo in June 1964; it was to be attended by the

Prime Ministers of Malaysia, Indonesia and the Philippines (whose Government supported Indonesia, and who had also broken off diplomatic relations with Malaysia) in an effort to resolve the problems of the Confrontation. In the event the talks proved a complete failure, and their breakdown was the signal for Indonesia to renew her guerrilla offensive. The first serious incident took place within twenty-four hours of the breakdown of the Tokyo talks, when the 1/6th Gurkha Rifles came under heavy attack by a regular Indonesian force at Rasau in Sarawak. The Gurkhas lost five killed and had five wounded, which represented a severe reversal for them.

During July 1964 no fewer than thirty-four major attacks were launched by the Indonesians, mostly against Gurkha troops, but the latter sustained minimal casualties and in each case the raiders were beaten off. By this time it was clear that the situation had deteriorated far beyond mere confrontation with guerrilla bands, and on 17 August a serious threat developed when about 100 Indonesian soldiers went ashore at three separate points in Johore, on the west coast of Peninsular Malaysia. Ten days later, Indonesian commandos carried out an attack on the Esso Island bunkering station off Singapore, and an Indonesian Navy flotilla attacked a Malaysian patrol craft. Then, on 2 September, an AURI C-130 dropped ninety-six paratroops near Labis in north central Johore. The C-130 was not intercepted, and its mission led to fears that AURI might now attempt to attack the RAF's Singapore bases and the RAAF station at Butterworth. FEAF's reaction was to call all its strike/attack squadrons to a state of alert, first of all to deal with the Indonesian forces operating on the Malaysian mainland.

The Hunter pilots of No 20 Squadron, tasked with providing air support for the ground forces engaging the Indonesian paratroops (two battalions of the Royal Malay Regiment and a battalion of the Malaysian Rangers), had a difficult job, for the enemy was well-concealed in 1,000 square yards of jungle. The Hunters went into action on 3 September, following several hours on standby while the location of the enemy troops was established, and the squadron flew a total of fourteen sorties, its aircraft armed with sixteen 3-inch rocket projectiles with semi-armour-piercing warheads and full loads of 30 mm ammunition. The strikes lasted several days, and during the attacks the Hunter pilots used a line of discarded enemy parachutes, still hanging in the treetops, as an aiming point in the hope of hitting the elusive Indonesians or destroying their supplies. The air strikes undoubtedly had a very demoralizing effect on the Indonesian soldiers, forcing them to change their positions continually, and by the end of September all but two of them had been killed or captured.

This reverse, however, did not deter the Indonesians. Between 17 August 1964 and 29 March 1965 there were forty-one landings, attempted landings and sabotage operations in western Malaysia, involving at least 740 Indonesian personnel. Of these, 451 succeeded in landing on the Malaysian mainland; 142 were killed and 309 captured by the Security Forces. On 23 December 1964, the Hunters of No 20 Squadron joined forces with the Canberras of No 45 Squadron in an air strike operation codenamed BIRDSONG, in which the aircraft carried out real and simulated attacks in an effort to demoralize the infiltrators and compel them to split into smaller groups that could be more readily tackled by the Security Forces. The attacks were repeated on 24 and 26 December and were directed by a Forward Air Controller in a Whirlwind helicopter of No 103 Squadron. (Later, in 1969, the squadron had its own flight of Pioneer aircraft for forward air control duties, making it unique in the RAF in this respect.)

By this time the threat from Indonesia was being taken very seriously indeed by HM Government. Since December 1963, detachments of the V-bomber force of RAF Bomber Command had been sent to Tengah and to RAAF Butterworth on a regular basis to act as a deterrent to an escalation of Indonesia's hostile intentions; the aircraft involved were mainly Handley Page Victors of Nos 15, 55 and 57 Squadrons. The Victor, together with the Vulcan, formed Britain's strategic nuclear deterrent force in the early 1960s, but it could also carry a formidable load of twenty-one 1,000 lb. conventional bombs, which could have wrought considerable damage on Indonesian industrial and military installations if such action had proven necessary. In September 1964, as an insurance against possible Indonesian air strikes, the Victors of No 57 Squadron were retained at Tengah beyond the normal period of their detachment.

The presence of the Victors almost certainly deterred the Indonesians from any thoughts of using their Tu-16s in an offensive role against Malaysia. The air defences were also strengthened in September 1964 by the arrival of eight Javelins of No 64 Squadron from RAF Binbrook, while No 65 (SAM) Squadron, whose Bloodhound Mk II surface-to-air missiles had been undergoing tropical trials at RAF Seletar, was ordered to bring one of its missile sections to immediate operational readiness and prepare to defend Singapore. All these resources were put to the test in a full-scale air defence exercise which took place on 28 October.

Meanwhile, attacks by Indonesian regular forces of up to company strength had continued against Sabah and Sarawak throughout the summer of 1964, the enemy having established a chain of jungle bases just inside Kalimantan. It was apparent to General Walker that these bases would have to be destroyed, or at least pushed well back from the border, if the situation was to be brought under control. Walker made strong representation to Admiral Sir Varyl Begg, the Commander-in-Chief Far East, who in turn made repeated requests to the British

Government for authority to extend harassing attacks across the border. The strict prohibition on 'hot pursuit' into Kalimantan had not greatly inconvenienced the Security Forces in the early stages of the campaign, but it was now denying them many opportunities to follow up and destroy raiding parties. In the end London relented, but only to the extent that the Security Forces were now permitted to undertake 'hot pursuit' operations to a depth of 3,000 yards into Kalimantan. Such operations could only be undertaken on the condition that they left no evidence, such as civilian casualties or damage, which might enable Indonesia to level a charge of aggression against the Security Forces. In addition, friendly artillery was now permitted to open fire on Indonesian mortar batteries across the border, but only in self-defence.

By the end of 1964, however, with the breakdown of successive peace talks and no negotiated settlement to the Confrontation in sight, the British Government and those Commonwealth Governments supporting the campaign in Borneo were becoming increasingly concerned by the drain on their defence resources and by the levels of expenditure being incurred. The politico-military dilemma was acute, for if the situation were allowed to escalate and get out of hand it might result in open and declared warfare, which the Commonwealth Governments wished to avoid at all costs. Nevertheless, Indonesian provocation had reached a level at which a defensive policy based entirely on non-retaliation was no longer acceptable. The British Government therefore authorized the Commander-in-Chief Far East to carry out offensive patrol operations up to a depth of 10,000 yards into Kalimantan, and to attack any suitable targets found in the operational area. As before, the strictest control was to be exercised over these operations, and all measures were to be taken to ensure that the fact that they were taking place did not become general knowledge.

The cross-border operations, codenamed CLARET, became effective in their extended form on 13 January 1965. The start of the operations coincided with intelligence that Indonesia was substantially increasing her forces in Kalimantan, and to strengthen his own forces the Director of Operations received two additional infantry battalions, the 2nd Battalion The Parachute Regiment and the 1st Battalion The Argyll and Sutherland Highlanders, which he allotted to the First Division of Sarawak. At the same time, the Australian and New Zealand Governments authorized their combat units to be deployed in eastern Malaysia, and a battalion of the Royal Australian Regiment with the 1st (Australian) SAS Squadron and the 1st (New Zealand) Ranger Squadron were added to the reinforcements.

This influx of new forces greatly increased the demand for air-supply and trooplifting operations, and to assist with these No 230 Squadron, with Whirlwind Mk 10 helicopters, was deployed at Labuan from RAF

Odiham in March 1965. One of the principal helicopter tasks was to change over the battalions and other units in the Forward Defence Locations (FDL) along the frontier. As there was no room for more than one unit in an FDL, the outgoing unit had to depart in the helicopters which brought in its replacement. The procedure was that the replacement unit would be flown into Labuan or Kuching early in the day by Argosy, Hastings or Beverley transport aircraft and transferred immediately to Belvedere or Whirlwind helicopters, which would then fly to the FDL, unload the incoming battalion and uplift the outgoing one. By the time the helicopters completed the lift back to the base airfield the medium-range transports would have been refuelled and made ready to load the troops, so that a complete battalion airlift of several hundred men between the FDL in Borneo and Singapore could be completed in a single day.

Apart from trooplifting, the twin-rotor Belvedere helicopters of No 66 Squadron RAF and the Wessex helicopters of the Royal Navy – especially those of No 846 Squadron, which became eastern Malaysia's 'resident' naval helicopter unit – performed valuable service in the heavy lift task. The Wessex could carry an underslung load of up to 4,000 lb., while the Belvedere could lift 5,250 lb., making it possible to carry a 105 mm howitzer. Only a limited number of these very important guns were deployed in Borneo, and their rapid transport from site to site by helicopter was vital. In this task the Belvederes operated in pairs, one carrying the gun and the other its ammunition. Both loads were lowered into a previously planned position, the gun ranged on to a target and fired within minutes, after which they could be transferred to another site several miles away, the helicopters flying at treetop height to escape detection. These tactics led the enemy to believe that the ground forces possessed far more artillery support than was actually the case. The Belvedere could also carry an anti-mortar radar detector, which tracked the flight of a 3-inch mortar bomb and plotted its firing position with great accuracy and enabled the ground forces to return the fire, often while the enemy bomb was still in flight. This equipment, too, could be moved rapidly from site to site.

There was no let-up in Indonesian pressure on Peninsular Malaysia during the early months of 1965, and the Singapore defences remained at a high alert state. During this period the Hunters of No 20 Squadron were continually involved in the close support of ground forces engaged in mopping up pockets of infiltrators, and in flying reconnaissance missions along the coastline.

On the night of 30/31 May 1965, twenty-five regular Indonesian troops landed on the south coast of east Johore near Tanjong Pen-Gelih, only seven miles east of Changi. The group encamped in some old Japanese wartime fortifications, which they intended to turn into a firm base while they awaited the arrival of reinforcements. The whole force would then split up and move to Kelantan, where the Indonesians planned to contact and train 'dissident groups'.

Troops of the Royal Malay Regiment failed to dislodge the enemy and suffered casualties, so four Hunters of No 20 Squadron were called in to do the job. Directed by a Forward Air Controller, they made rocket attacks on the fortifications and followed these up with cannon attacks. No casualties were inflicted on the Indonesians, but under the intensity of the air attacks they were forced to abandon their positions and were rounded up during the next few days, one of them being killed.

This Indonesian infiltration was part of a sustained offensive that had been in progress since April 1965, and which was seen as a prelude to a forthcoming Afro-Asian Conference which was expected to be held in Algiers in June. The Indonesian Government planned to use the conference as a platform to further its cause, and it wished to do so from a position of strength by seeking to gain military success in Malaysia. The new offensive began in the early hours of 27 April 1965, when a strong Indonesian force launched a heavy night attack on Plaman Mapu in the First Division of Sarawak, which was held by Company HQ and an under-strength platoon of B Company of the 2nd Battalion The Parachute Regiment.

The Indonesian assault was supported by light mortars and rocket launchers, the attackers storming the HQ's thinly-defended perimeter and succeeding in gaining a small foothold inside the barbed wire defences. There followed ninety minutes of savage close-quarter combat in which both sides fought with great gallantry, the Indonesians being highly-trained troops; at one point the British Company Sergeant-Major seized a machine-gun from a wounded paratrooper and rallied his men by standing up and emptying a magazine of ammunition into the enemy at almost point-blank range. The Indonesians were eventually dislodged and reinforcements were quickly flown to the scene by the Whirlwind helicopters of No 225 Squadron. The Parachute Regiment lost two men killed and eight wounded in the action, but inflicted an estimated thirty casualties on the enemy. A measure of the Indonesians' determination was that they returned to the area repeatedly during the next fortnight, in parties between 30 and 200 strong. They were just as repeatedly ambushed by the Security Forces, notably the 2nd Parachute Regiment and the Argyll and Sutherland Highlanders, with artillery support provided by a field battery of the Royal Australian Artillery. In a series of actions lasting into June, the Security Forces killed or wounded an estimated forty-six Indonesians for the loss of only one paratrooper killed and one Argyll wounded.

By this time Major-General George Lea had succeeded General Walker as Director of Operations, and under his command cross-border operations were stepped up in an attempt to dominate the border area and also to deny the area beyond, extending some two miles into Kalimantan, to the Indonesian forces. Much preliminary work in this respect had been done by B and D Squadrons of 22nd Special Air Service Regiment. In January and February, B Squadron had crossed the frontier on several occasions in search of Indonesian staging camps and river lines of communication, which were much used by the Indonesians on their infiltrations. The SAS were authorized to take offensive action during the last two days of each patrol, provided that they were reasonably assured of success and that no incriminating documents were left behind.

In April, a patrol of D Squadron, having spent six days watching river craft on the Upper Koemba, sighted a boat crewed by Indonesian soldiers and ambushed them, shooting two and killing a third with grenades, and in May, another patrol of D Squadron successfully ambushed a large troop launch, which caught fire, capsized and exploded with unknown casualties among its occupants.

In addition to ambushing river craft, the SAS also laid ambushes along jungle tracks, often using Claymore mines, which on exploding ejected 900 lethal steel balls over the surrounding area. In the early months of cross-border operations, the SAS located several enemy camps, and on occasions spent days being hunted in the jungle by Indonesian patrols as they withdrew. The information brought back by the 22nd SAS Regiment on the location and extent of the enemy's bases, the river routes used, the type of boats and the number of men in them, and the siting of suitable ambush points, was of enormous value in subsequent offensive operations. One patrol tapped an Indonesian telephone line several miles across the border, spending five days tape-recording enemy messages and narrowly escaping capture by a patrol of Indonesian paratroops; another, in the course of a dawn skirmish, snatched important documents from a hut that was being used as an advanced HQ by the enemy.

The increase in Indonesian incursions across the border during 1965 was also accompanied by an increased number of penetrations by Indonesian aircraft, although these usually involved short-range flights into Malaysian territory, and by the time the RAF's Hunters or Javelins arrived at the scene in response to a reported violation the intruder had usually slipped back into Indonesian territory. On one occasion, however, a Javelin must have given the crew of an Indonesian C-130 a nasty shock when it passed the transport head-on in a valley, with barely 100 feet clearance between the two aircraft. By the time the Javelin turned to intercept, the C-130 had made good its escape. Despite problems such as these, the RAF fighter force at Labuan and Kuching scrambled its Battle Flight in response to every reported intrusion, and there can be no doubt that the rapid reaction of the Hunters and Javelins deterred the Indonesians from making deeper penetrations.

The principal base in Borneo for fighter–strike operations was Labuan, which had a long runway and which, as it was situated on an offshore island, was relatively secure from surprise attack or sabotage. In 1962 it was nothing more than a staging post, managed by seventy-eight airmen detached from Changi, but over the next three years it was rapidly developed and expanded until in the spring of 1965 it had an establishment of over 1,000 personnel on a one-year unaccompanied tour. Being situated at the centre of the Air Defence Identification Zone, it was well placed for rapid response to Indonesian overflights, the Hunters and Javelins maintaining high states of readiness by day and night. Much of this was boring work, and when fighters were scrambled and managed to obtain a sighting the suspect aircraft usually turned out to be friendly; occasional sightings of Indonesian types were mostly at long range, as the target sped back to the sanctuary of its own territory.

While in Borneo, the fighter detachments (which occasionally included the Hunters of No 28 Squadron, based in Hong Kong) were operationally responsible to the Commander, Air Forces Borneo, whose HQ was at Labuan and who was in turn responsible to the Commander, British Forces Borneo. The squadrons' main tasks throughout their operational deployments were to maintain round-the-clock operational readiness states, to fly low-level patrols over the territory of Sabah and Sarawak, both to deter possible intruders and to boost the morale of the local population (the sorties were known as 'Flag Waves'), and also to act as fighter escort to Hastings, Argosy, Beverley and Valetta aircraft engaged in supply-dropping operations to Commonwealth forces in the interior. Fighter escort was the most interesting task of all, and the fighter pilots were full of admiration for the skill displayed by the transport crews, operating at speeds close to the stall inside frighteningly narrow valleys to ensure that their loads went down accurately on the dropping zones.

The weather was a constant problem, particularly for the detachments at Kuching, where tropical storms could blow up with no more than a few minutes' warning. Labuan enjoyed a longer warning period, and if necessary pilots could divert to one of two other airfields, Brunei and Jesselton.

In addition to the RAF units mentioned above, the Far East Air Force had two more strike and one fighter squadrons at its disposal. The strike squadrons, both equipped with Canberras, were No 2 RAAF at Butterworth and No 14 RNZAF on Singapore; the fighter squadron, No 77 RAAF, was equipped with F-86 Sabres and was deployed at Labuan during various periods of the Confrontation. All these units added to the powerful air forces' deterrent contribution.

Flying in support of the campaign in eastern Malaysia, RAF and Royal Navy helicopter pilots displayed considerable skill and courage, particularly in the casualty evacuation role. One such outstanding mission, for example, was carried out in the afternoon of 28 February 1965 by Flying Officer D. T. J. Collinson, a Whirlwind pilot with No 225 Squadron at Kuching. Collinson and his crew, Flying Officer H. B. Lake and Senior Aircraftman M. N. Dyet, took off in search of two British soldiers, both of them wounded, in the jungle. One of the men was known to be so badly injured that he would almost certainly die unless he reached hospital quickly.

One of the wounded men had a radio beacon, and Collinson managed to make a reasonably accurate pinpoint of his location. He passed on the information to a ground patrol, who picked up the soldier some time later. The air search was resumed at first light the next morning and Collinson quickly found the patrol, which was carrying the wounded man on a stretcher. However, the trees were too close together and too high to allow him either to land or to lower a cable. Realizing that there was nothing more he could do for the time being, the pilot carried on his search for the second soldier, who was located in deep jungle.

Collinson found the man and backed the helicopter's tail between two trees, hovering over him. As he did so, Indonesian troops opened up with small arms fire from some distance away. Despite the danger, the pilot held the Whirlwind steady until the soldier was able to attach himself to the rescue harness before being lifted safely aboard. By this time it was dusk and Collinson completed the flight home in pitch darkness, making a detour to avoid a thunderstorm before landing the casualty at Kuching Hospital. The next morning, the second soldier was also picked up from a clearing where the patrol had taken him. Both men subsequently made a full recovery.

In the summer and autumn of 1965, Security Forces operations took an increasing toll of the enemy on and beyond the frontier. The brunt of the fighting was borne by the 1/2nd, 2/2nd, 2/6th and 2/7th Gurkhas and by the Royal Marines of 40 and 42 Commandos, but successful actions were also fought by the Scots Guards and the 2nd and 3rd Green Jackets. The 2nd Green Jackets killed forty-three enemy for the loss of only one man, while their 3rd Battalion claimed eight Indonesian dead and five wounded.

Other regiments, including the Durham Light Infantry, the King's Own Scottish Borderers and the Gordon Highlanders, sent battalions to Borneo on operational tours. All faced the same common enemies: highly-trained Indonesian regular troops, extreme tropical conditions, swarms of mosquitoes and – perhaps worst of all – legions of rats. An excellent description of life on patrol in the jungle, with its attendant dangers, is given by Major Ian Uzell, then a 2nd Lieutenant with 40 Commando Royal Marines:

'The section would be divided into two small units. Three men would be sent out in the morning, then the remaining four or five in the afternoon or evening. So it was, that on 20 February, the section was split, and L-Corp Davis, Jim Gooding and myself found ourselves on a routine patrol to search random "bashas". We came across one in particular which the owner (a Chinese) did not appear keen for us to investigate. With an uneasy feeling, Jim and Davis inspected it while I kept watch with the Bren gun . . . .

'About 10.30 we heard what we thought was gunfire in the distance, because sound travels for miles, but bamboo cracking has a similar sound, so we couldn't make our minds up at first. Then came a couple of deep explosions and we put this down to hand grenades. Confirmation of this came from the villagers themselves, when they put the shutters over their windows, which were normally open . . . . Oggie Howes came back with the news that they had been caught in a fight and that Cpl Chapple had been killed and the rest seriously wounded at the same Chinese basha. Oggie himself was wounded, with several bullets in his arms, which were taken out by the medic. A radio message was relayed to Company HQ and it was decided to send a helicopter to the village at once, even though this entailed flying in the dark, and it duly arrived with torches being used as landing lights. The plan was to try and bring the wounded back to the village and so get them to hospital quicker. Things did not work out this way, though, as it was up to the rest of us to effect a rescue and decide what to do when we got there. The rescue party consisted of 2-Lt Christie Miller, L-Corp Davis, Jim Gooding, myself and Oggie Howes, who insisted on going back. Well, anyone who has been in the jungle at night would know how pitch black it is, and so as not to get separated we decided to tie a length of rope onto the back of our belts, which was held fairly taut by the man behind; this enabled us to keep some distance between ourselves, but keep in contact at the same time. There was the added danger of coming under fire from the enemy if they decided to ambush us on the main track while effecting the rescue.

'After what seemed like hours, we finally reached the basha about 01.30 and saw for ourselves the fight the lads had put up. They had the Chinese owner whom we had spoken to earlier in the day as a prisoner. The place was an absolute wreck, bullet-holes were evident all over and the back-room walls had gaping holes in them, no doubt from the hand grenades. Jim started to attend to the wounded, Scouse's legs were bleeding badly, Jock Balderstone had arm wounds but seemed in good spirits and morphine was given to them both to ease the pain. Not so for Jock Findley though, as he had several bullets in his chest and was coughing blood . . . Reg Chapple was in a small room and nothing else could be done until the morning when the helicopter could land and evacuate the wounded . . . .

'The enemy had retreated and the only sign we could see were bloodstains leading into the jungle, so they had at least some wounded. We had radioed our position to the rest of the company, and at first light came the helicopter and both the Troops' other sections on foot led by Cpls Bell and Mick Fulton, with some Iban tribesmen who quickly set off in pursuit of the enemy. The helicopter left within minutes of landing and quiet returned again.

'A police patrol arrived on foot with some more Iban tribesmen and started to interrogate the Chinese, and after searching his out-buildings found the rest of his family. It turned out that he was harbouring twenty Indonesians and admitted that the three Marines who had first searched his place in the day were being watched by them all the time. He was led away and we returned to Sekembal once more for some rest.'

The jungle war in Borneo brought the award of one Victoria Cross. It was awarded to Lance-Corporal Rambahadur Limbu of C Company, 2/10th Gurkhas, for a particularly gallant action during a cross-border patrol from the Bau District of Sarawak. C Company located an enemy force strongly entrenched in platoon strength on top of a sheer hill; the only approach route was along a knife-edge ridge allowing no more than three men to move abreast. Rambahadur, leading his support group, saw the nearest enemy in a trench, armed with a machine-gun. The Indonesian opened fire from ten yards, killing one Gurkha. Rambahadur charged the trench and killed the machine-gunner, whereupon intense fire from the whole enemy position was directed on his newly-won position. Realizing that he was unable to support his platoon from this point, Rambahadur courageously left the comparative safety of his trench and, disregarding the hail of fire directed at him, returned to his support group and led them to a better position some yards ahead. He then tried to indicate his intentions to his platoon commander but, such was the noise of battle, this proved impossible. He therefore moved into the open and reported personally, despite the extreme danger of being hit both by the enemy and the other Gurkhas.

As he was reporting he saw that two men of his own group had been seriously wounded. Knowing the fearful repercussions of leaving any soldier, dead or alive, on Indonesian soil, he made three attempts to rescue them, rescuing one man at the second attempt and the second man at the third. The enemy did their utmost to prevent him. The last attempt was made in a series of short rushes and at one point Rambahadur was pinned down for some minutes by the intense and accurate automatic fire which could be seen striking the ground all around him. For all but a few seconds of the twenty minutes that this action lasted, Rambahadur had been moving alone in full view of the enemy and under the continuous aimed fire of their automatic weapons. His citation stated:

> That he was able to achieve what he did against such overwhelming odds, without being hit, is miraculous. His outstanding personal bravery, selfless conduct, complete contempt of the enemy and determination to save the lives of the men of his fire group set an incomparable example and inspired all who saw him.

The whole battle lasted an hour, at point-blank range and with the utmost ferocity shown by both sides. When it ended, at least twenty-four Indonesians were dead; the Gurkhas lost three killed and two wounded.

Up to the beginning of 1965 the principal infantry weapons used by the Security Forces in eastern Malaysia were the L1A1 7.62 mm self-loading rifle (SLR), the Vickers medium machine-gun and the Bren light machine-gun. The L1A1 SLR was not suitable for jungle warfare, being intended for use in the NATO area of operations, and in 1965 it was replaced in Borneo by the 5.56 mm M16 Armalite assault rifle, which had been designed for close-quarter and jungle warfare. It was light, weighing eight and a half pounds with a full magazine of twenty rounds, and had a practical rate of fire of up to sixty rounds per minute; the L1A1, by comparison, weighed over eleven pounds with a twenty-round magazine and had a practical rate of fire of forty rounds per minute. The Armalite was received thankfully by the Security Forces, particularly in view of the fact that the Indonesians were already using it.

The Bren and Vickers machine-guns were also replaced by the much more effective 7.62 mm general purpose machine-gun (GPMG), a fully automatic, belt-fed, gas-operated weapon that could continue firing for a considerable period, although the Bren continued in use for some time for patrol work because it was lighter and more manageable. The old 3-inch mortar, too, was replaced by the 81 mm, and the 3.5-inch rocket launcher by the Swedish-designed 84 mm Carl Gustav anti-tank weapon, which was devastating when used against boats and buildings. Other innovations included a device named TOBIAS (Terrestrial Oscillation Battlefield Intruder Alarm System) which, using seismic sensors, could detect a person at 50 yards; it was installed beyond the perimeters of border forts to detect the approach of the enemy.

The second half of 1965 was dominated by political events. First of all, Singapore left the Malaysian Federation under a separation agreement, but Singaporean troops continued to serve in Borneo and the withdrawal made no difference to the British military presence on the island. Of far greater significance was the Djakarta coup of 30 September, when the Indonesian Communist Party attempted to seize power and a number of senior Army officers were killed. A nationwide anti-Communist reaction followed, and in the ensuing political turbulence President Soekarno was removed from power.

This had no immediate effect on the Confrontation, but it was noticeable that Indonesia's new leaders were not allowing the situation to escalate. There no longer appeared to be the will or intention to mount large-scale and determined incursions. According to a report to the Chief of the Defence Staff in London from the then Commander-in-Chief, Far East, Air Chief Marshal Sir John Grandy, the decline in Indonesian military activity was due to the following factors:

a. The very real fear of retaliatory action which the United Kingdom might take against Indonesian forces should they be ordered to make large-scale incursions, particularly against western Malaysia.
b. The effective methods employed against infiltration in both east and west Malaysia.
c. With certain notable exceptions, the poor showing of Indonesian forces, both regular and irregular, in operations.
d. Logistic and maintenance difficulties.
e. Lack of sympathy with Indonesia among the Malaysian peoples.

By the end of 1965 the Commonwealth forces in Borneo were in a very strong defensive position, and were inflicting growing casualties on the enemy. Operations continued into 1966, and in March that year the 1/10th Gurkhas, who had relieved the 2/10th in the Bau District of Sarawak, killed thirty-seven Indonesians in a classically-executed ambush for no loss to themselves. It was the most spectacular success of the campaign, and also virtually the last, although hostilities continued on a small scale right up to 11 August 1966, when, after several months of negotiation, Malaysia and Indonesia signed a peace treaty in Bangkok, bringing the Confrontation to an end three years and eight months after it had begun.

During that time, total Commonwealth losses had amounted to 114 killed and 180 wounded, a figure that included 43 Gurkhas killed and 87 wounded, 16 Royal Marines killed and 20 wounded, and the infantry battalions 16 killed and 51 wounded. The Indonesians officially admitted a loss of 600 men killed, but the total was almost certainly higher as a result of the Security Forces' cross-border operations, which officially never took place.

The political significance of the campaign in Borneo was that it preserved the independence of Malaysia and almost certainly prevented the spread of Communism into Indonesia, with far-reaching consequences for the rest of South-East Asia. In military terms, there was one major lesson to be derived from the campaign, summed up admirably by the Air Officer Commanding, No 224 Group (the former AHQ Malaya).

> There can be no doubt of the validity of one major lesson learned from the Confrontation. Adequate tactical air forces, supported by strategic air power and properly trained, handled and operated in close partnership with the ground forces, are as essential and critical a factor in a successful military campaign today as ever before. If our future national policy envisages the conduct of, or participation in such operations in the future, this fact can only be forgotten or ignored at our peril.

Appendix 1

NAVAL FORCES IN THE EMERGENCY AND CONFRONTATION

Although this work has been primarily concerned with the land campaigns in Malaya and Borneo, and their associated tactical air support, the role of the Royal Navy in both was a prominent one. During the Emergency, warships of the Royal Navy and the Royal Malayan Navy played a vital part in patrolling the sea approaches, preventing arms and supplies from reaching the insurgents; naval guns bombarded terrorist camps in the jungle, and assault landing craft fitted out as gunboats operated in the Malayan rivers. The islands off the east coast of Malaya had always been a haven for illegal immigrants, and when the Emergency began the dangers of this immigration and the possibility of smuggling arms and equipment to the terrorists by sea greatly increased.

Illegal immigrants came from anywhere on the China coast up to Hainan and crossed the Gulf of Siam in small craft, usually junks, especially during the period of the north-east monsoon. Reaching the islands off the east coast of Malaya they would lie up on the lee shore during daylight and wait for nightfall to make the final crossing to the mainland.

As it was impossible for the Royal Navy to keep constant watch on all these islands along the full length of the Malayan coastline, a system of combined patrols was initiated using one sloop or destroyer and one aircraft (an RAF Sunderland) which covered pre-determined areas depending on whatever intelligence was available on the likely movements of illegal immigrants. 'Blue Water' patrols covered a 100-mile stretch of coastline and an area extending 80 miles out to sea in order to intercept any craft attempting to run directly for the mainland, while 'Coastal and Island' patrols monitored inlets and anchorages in the Tioman Island group, the southern tip of the Johore coast and the islands off the north-east coast of Trengganu and Kelantan. In 1951 nine regular combined patrols were being mounted each week off the Malayan coast, but by then the danger of illegal immigration was well under control and there were no attempts to smuggle arms to the terrorists by sea, so patrols were reduced to one or two a week for the remainder of the Emergency.

During the Confrontation with Indonesia the Royal Navy lent powerful logistical support, with aircraft carriers providing floating bases and a variety of other support vessels almost continuously ferrying battalions of Commonwealth troops and items of equipment, including light aircraft and helicopters, to the operational area. Around the coast of northern Borneo, warships and small armed motor-boats manned by the Royal Navy maintained incessant patrols of offshore approaches and rivers vulnerable to infiltration by sea, while the primary task was to guard the western coastline of Malaysia against attempted infiltration by groups of Indonesian regular soldiers and saboteurs. This task was complicated by the barter trade which continued between the Indonesian islands, Malaya and Singapore, and by the fishing craft present in large numbers in the Malacca and Singapore straits. During the peak period of the Confrontation, British and Commonwealth warships were continuously on patrol in the straits for over 700 days and nights, and intercepted 90 per cent of known attempts to infiltrate. The burden of these patrols was borne by the small ships of the inshore flotillas, which spent an average of twenty-one days a month at sea. To augment patrols around the coast of Malaysia, coastal minesweepers and seaward defence boats were brought out of local reserve at Singapore, and were joined by Australian and New Zealand warships.

Appendix 2

COMMONWEALTH MILITARY AND AIR UNITS IN THE MALAYAN EMERGENCY

1st King's Dragoon Guards
4th Queen's Own Hussars
11th Hussars
12th Royal Lancers
13th/18th Royal Hussars
15th/19th The King's Royal Hussars
2nd Field Regiment RA
25th Field Regiment RA
26th Field Regiment RA
48th Field Regiment RA
1st Singapore Regiment RA
100 Field Battery RAA
101 Field Battery RAA
105 Field Battery RAA
11 Independent Field Squadron RE
50 Gurkha Field Regiment RE
51 Field Engineer Regiment RE
74 Field Park Squadron RE
410 Independent Plant Troop RE
17th (Gurkha) Signal Regiment
208 (Commonwealth) Signal Squadron
Malaya Command Signal Squadron
3rd Grenadier Guards
2nd Coldstream Guards
2nd Scots Guards
1st Bn The Queen's Royal Regiment
1st Bn The Royal Lincolnshire Regiment
1st Bn The Devonshire Regiment
1st Bn The Suffolk Regiment
1st Bn The Somerset Light Infantry
1st Bn The West Yorkshire Regiment
1st Bn The East Yorkshire Regiment

1st Bn The Green Howards
1st Bn The Royal Scots Fusiliers
1st Bn The Cheshire Regiment
1st Bn The Royal Welsh Fusiliers
1st Bn The South Wales Borderers
1st Bn The Cameronians
1st Bn The Royal Iniskilling Fusiliers
1st Bn The Worcestershire Regiment
1st Bn The Royal Hampshire Regiment
1st Bn The Sherwood Foresters
1st Bn The Loyal Regiment
1st Bn 3rd East Anglian Regiment
1st Bn The Queen's Own Royal West Kent Regiment
1st Bn The King's Own Yorkshire Light Infantry
1st Bn The Wiltshire Regiment
1st Bn The Manchester Regiment
1st Bn The Seaforth Highlanders
1st Bn The Gordon Highlanders
The Independent Parachute Squadron
40 Commando Royal Marines
42 Commando Royal Marines
45 Commando Royal Marines
1st/2nd King Edward VII's Own Gurkha Rifles
2nd/2nd King Edward VII's Own Gurkha Rifles
1st/6th Queen Elizabeth's Own Gurkha Rifles
1st/7th Duke of Edinburgh's Own Gurkha Rifles
1st/10th Princess Mary's Own Gurkha Rifles
2nd/10th Princess Mary's Own Gurkha Rifles
1st Bn The Rifle Brigade
22nd Special Air Service Regiment
1st Bn The King's African Rifles
3rd Bn The King's African Rifles
1st Bn The Northern Rhodesia Regiment
1st Bn The Fiji Infantry Regiment
1st Bn The Royal Australian Regiment
2nd Bn The Royal Australian Regiment
3rd Bn The Royal Australian Regiment
The Rhodesia Squadron, Special Air Service
The New Zealand Squadron, Special Air Service
1st Singapore Infantry Regiment
1st Bn The New Zealand Regiment
2nd Bn The New Zealand Regiment
1st Bn The Malay Regiment
2nd Bn The Malay Regiment

3rd Bn The Malay Regiment
4th Bn The Malay Regiment
5th Bn The Malay Regiment
6th Bn The Malay Regiment
7th Bn The Malay Regiment
The Royal Air Force Regiment (Malaya)

OFFENSIVE AIR SUPPORT SQUADRONS

No 1 RAAF
No 2 RAAF
No 3 RAAF
No 14 RNZAF
No 28 RAF
No 33 RAF
No 45 RAF
No 60 RAF
No 75 RNZAF
No 77 RAAF
No 84 RAF
No 88 RAF
No 205 RAF
No 209 RAF (to December 1954)

AIR TRANSPORT SUPPORT SQUADRONS

No 38 RAAF
No 41 RNZAF
No 48 RAF
No 52 RAF
No 110 RAF
No 155 RAF
No 194 RAF
No 209 RAF (from November 1958)
No 267 RAF
No 848 Naval Air Squadron
No 1311 Transport Flight
HQ Far East Transport Wing
Far East Communications Squadron
No 656 RAF (No 656 Squadron Army Air Corps from 1 September 1957)

PHOTOGRAPHIC RECONNAISSANCE SQUADRONS

No 81 RAF
The Malayan Auxiliary Air Force
Casualty Evacuation Flight, FEAF

BIBLIOGRAPHY

Barber, Noel, *War of the Running Dogs*, London: Collins, 1971.
Beaver, Paul, *Today's Royal Marines*, London: Patrick Stephens, 1988.
Campbell, Arthur, *Jungle Green*, London: Allen & Unwin, 1953.
Chapman, F. Spencer, *The Jungle is Neutral*, London: Chatto & Windus, 1949.
Clutterbuck, Richard, *The Long Long War*, London: Cassell, 1966.
Dewar, Michael, *Brush Fire Wars*, London: Robert Hale, 1984.
Gullick, J.M., *Malaya*, London: Ernest Benn, 1963.
Hampshire, A. Cecil, *The Royal Navy Since 1945*, 1975.
Hanrahan, Gene Z., *Communist Struggle in Malaya*, Washington: Institute of Public Relations, 1954.
Henniker, M.C.A., *Red Shadow Over Malaya*, London: Blackwood, 1955.
Jackson, Robert, *Strike from the Sea*, London: Barker, 1970.
——*The Dragonflies*, London: Barker, 1971.
——*Canberra: The Operational Record*, Shrewsbury: Airlife, 1989.
——*Hawker Hunter: The Operational Record*, Shrewsbury: Airlife, 1989.
Ladd, James D., *SAS Operations*, London: Robert Hale, 1986.
Lee, Sir David, *Eastward*, London: HMSO, 1984.
Majdalaney, Fred, *State of Emergency*, London: Longmans Green, 1962.
Miers, Richard, *Shoot to Kill*, London: Faber & Faber, 1959.
Miller, Harry, *Menace in Malaya*, London: Harrap, 1954.
——*Jungle War in Malaya*, London: Barker, 1972.
Mountbatten, Earl, of Burma, *South-East Asia 1943–45* (Report to the Combined Chiefs of Staff), London: HMSO, 1951.
Neillands, Robin, *By Sea and By Land*, London: Weidenfeld, 1987.
Nichol, Gladys, *Malaysia and Singapore*, London: Batsford, 1977.
O'Ballance, Edgar, *Malaya: The Communist Insurgent War*, London: Faber & Faber, 1966.
Oldfield, J.B., *The Green Howards in Malaya*, London: Gale & Polden, 1953.
Paget, Julian, *Counter-Insurgency Campaigning*, London: Faber & Faber, 1967.
Purcell, Victor, *The Chinese in Malaya*, Oxford: Oxford University Press, 1948.
Seymour, William, *British Special Forces*, London: Sidgwick & Jackson, 1985.
Tucci, Sandro, *Gurkhas*, London: Hamish Hamilton, 1985.

OFFICIAL DOCUMENTS CONSULTED (PRINCIPAL SOURCES ONLY)

Director of Operations (Malaya) Annual Reviews, 1950–9
Annual Reports on the Federation of Malaya (Colonial Office)
The Fight Against Communist Terrorism in Malaya, Central Office of Information, 1951
Monthly Command Summaries of RAF Contribution to Operation FIREDOG (AHB, RAF)
Intelligence Summaries issued by the Security Forces in Malaya

INDEX